AF266854

Light vs. Darkness

A Call to Come Out of Spiritual Darkness
and Walk in the Truth of Jesus Christ

Evangelist Martha P. Davis

Light vs. Darkness

A Call to Come Out of Spiritual Darkness
and Walk in the Truth of Jesus Christ

Evangelist Martha P. Davis

ISBN: 978-1-965943-20-5

This book is dedicated

to

God the Father

God the Son

And

God, the Holy Spirit

Introduction

It is with reverence, humility, and thanksgiving unto Almighty God that this collection of sermons by Evangelist Martha P. Davis is presented to you. These messages are not merely words spoken in a moment of time, but living testimonies of the unchanging truth of the gospel of Jesus Christ—the truth that pierces darkness, awakens the soul, and calls humanity back into fellowship with its Creator.

In an age where confusion abounds and the lines between truth and error have become increasingly blurred, the voice of the gospel must yet cry out with clarity and power. These sermons echo that cry. They are rooted deeply in the Word of God and carried by a burden that reflects the very heart of the Father—a heart that longs for all people to come into the knowledge of truth and be saved.

Throughout these pages, you will encounter a consistent and urgent theme: the call to come out of darkness and walk in the light. Evangelist Davis speaks with conviction and spiritual authority, reminding us that light is not an abstract concept, but a person—Jesus Christ, the Son of the living God. In Him is life, and that life is the light of men. Apart from Him, there is only darkness, confusion, and separation from the divine purpose for which we were created.

These sermons were birthed out of prayer, scripture, and a deep sensitivity to the leading of the Holy Spirit. They are both instructional and exhortational—teaching the truth while also compelling the listener and reader to respond. You will find within them a call to repentance, a call to holiness, a call to spiritual awareness, and above all, a call to love God with the whole heart.

Evangelist Davis does not present a softened or compromised message. Rather, she proclaims the gospel as it is written—boldly, faithfully, and without apology. She reminds us that Jesus Christ did not speak of Himself, but declared the will of the Father, and in the same spirit, these sermons seek not to glorify man, but to lift up the name of the Lord.

As you read, you will be challenged to examine your own heart. Are you walking in the light, or have you allowed areas of darkness to remain? Are you abiding in truth, or have you been swayed by the spirit of this age? These are not questions to be taken lightly, for the Word of God reveals that the time is drawing near when all must give account.

Yet within this urgency, there is also great hope.

For the same God who calls us out of darkness is the God who receives us with mercy. The same Christ who exposes sin is the One who forgives, restores, and transforms. The light does not come to condemn, but to save—to lead us into understanding, peace, and everlasting life.

This book is an invitation.

An invitation to hear.
An invitation to believe.
An invitation to return.
An invitation to draw nearer to God while there is yet time.

May these sermons stir your spirit, strengthen your faith, and lead you into a deeper walk with the Lord Jesus Christ. And may the light of the glorious gospel shine upon you, guiding your path now and into eternity. To God be all the glory.

Table of Contents

Light vs. Darkness I

First Aired Nov 24th, 1998

Glory, hallelujah. We give God the glory for being on the air today, and we thank God for the opportunity to come your way again. We thank God for all the things that He's doing in our lives, the manifold blessings of the Lord. He is such a good God. No matter what one would think of Him, He is the goodness that we are seeking. And I would urge everyone to turn to the true and living God, because He is good.

And the Lord is for humanity. His heartthrob is for humanity. The Word of God tells us in a favorite chapter, I'm sure, unto everyone that has read or heard the scriptures in Saint John 3, for God so loved the world that He gave His only begotten Son that whosoever would believe on Him should not perish, but have everlasting life.

And it is so true. And we that are born again, we that have received Jesus Christ as our Savior and Lord and friend, we know that God loves us so much, and we are trying to get that Word out to everyone, everyone that would hear it, everyone that would listen, everyone that would have faith to believe the truth. Pilate asked generations ago, what is truth? It's not what is, it's who is.

Jesus Christ declared of Himself, I am the way, the truth, and the life. Glory to God in the highest. Bow with me in prayer.

Precious Father, before the throne of grace, we come boldly as you've given us the privilege in Jesus Christ, our precious Lord's name. And we know that whatsoever we ask the Father in Jesus' name, we shall have it. You will grant it unto us.

And we're asking that by word will come forth under the action and the power of your Holy Spirit, my Savior and my God. Let those who are listening right now hear the Word of God. We know that time is coming to a close.

Glory to your name. And we're asking that the preaching of the gospel will go out into all the lands for Jesus' sake. For this cause, He came, not only to save those in His day when He was here on earth, but the gospel will be heard and believed by those that He would leave to preach and proclaim that which they had seen and that which they had heard.

And we are recipients of that precious gospel today. And we're asking that throughout all the world, the gospel of Jesus Christ will be preached because we know that Christ Jesus came, not speaking of Himself or preaching His own gospel, but all that you sent Him to say and do and proclaim. That has been accomplished.

And we are asking, Father, that those who are listening, you will bring into thy fold today, those that are outside of the arc of safety, those that are not saved, those that have not called on the name of your only begotten Son, Jesus. We're asking that you will receive them today as they humble themselves and call on your name. And all those who have known you as personal Savior, Lord, friend, and Father, we're asking that they will come closer, for surely it is time for us all to come closer unto you. We ask these petitions in the name of your Son, Jesus.

And we're asking, Lord God, that you would bind the powers of darkness, overthrow the intents of the wicked one, that we'll try to rob and steal from the people of God by sound counsel, by true word. We ask this in Jesus' name, amen and amen.

In the book of St. John, the seventh chapter, we see in the word of God. And Jesus, speaking of light, says in verse 15,

> *And the Jews marvelled, saying, How knoweth this man letters, having never learned? Jesus answered them, and said, My doctrine is not mine, but his that sent me. If any man will do his will, he shall know of the doctrine, whether it be of God, or whether I speak of myself. He that speaketh of himself seeketh his own glory: but he that seeketh his glory that sent him, the same is true, and no unrighteousness is in him.*

If any man will do his will, he shall know of the doctrine, whether it be of God, or whether I speak of myself. And this Jesus proclaimed throughout the time that he was allotted here on the face of this earth.

And I am speaking today concerning the light of the glorious gospel, and also the darkness of the wicked one. The word of God plainly tells us that we are to walk as children of the light and not to abide in darkness. Darkness blinds the mind, it closes the eyes, it causes the heart to be deceitful and deceived.

Light brings goodness and understanding; it brings knowledge and wisdom. It causes us to know the power of God, it increases our faith, and it causes us to commune with God, our maker. God tells us to abide in the light and walk as children of the day, that we might see where we are going.

In the book of St. John, chapter 7, the people strove with Jesus Christ. Some were wanting to believe, and as they heard Jesus Christ speak, they knew that no one had ever spoken like Jesus. And others said, Ah, he hath a devil, he deceives the people.

And Jesus plainly said, I have no devil. Why is it that you cannot receive my word? There is one that judgeth you. He said, I judge you not, but there is one that judgeth you, speaking of the Father.

Because God sent his only begotten Son to speak the mind of the Father, to declare the heart of the Father towards the children of men. And they refused to believe. And Jesus goes on to tell them,

> *Did not Moses give you the law, and yet none of you keepeth the law? Why go ye about to kill me?*

They actually wanted to kill Jesus because they did not know or perceive that this was the light, this was the Messiah, this was the promise of the Father.

They were not watching. They were not truly watching to hear the truth, to know it. You can only know the truth when you are looking for the truth. Verse 20,

> *The people answered and said, Thou hast a devil: who goeth about to kill thee? Jesus answered and said unto them, I have done one work, and ye all marvel. Moses therefore gave unto you circumcision; (not because it is of Moses, but of the fathers;) and ye on the sabbath day circumcise a man.*
>
> *If a man on the sabbath day receive circumcision, that the law of Moses should not be broken; are ye angry at me, because I have made a man every whit whole on the sabbath day? Judge not according to the appearance,*

don't judge me according to what it seems to be,

> *but judge righteous judgment.*

It's a good thing that I have done this deed to this man that was blind. This man that needed deliverance. I have brought deliverance because it is the will of God. He loves humanity. And I have come to present God's love and to manifest His love through good deeds unto the children of men. Why can you not see? Why call me a devil? Because I do that which is good.

> *Then said some of them of Jerusalem, Is not this he, whom they seek to kill? But, lo, he speaketh boldly, and they say nothing unto him. Do the rulers know indeed that this is the very Christ? Howbeit we*

*know this man whence he is: but when Christ
cometh, no man knoweth whence he is.*

*Then cried Jesus in the temple as he taught,
saying, Ye both know me, and ye know whence I am:
and I am not come of myself, but he that sent me is
true, whom ye know not. But I know him: for I am
from him, and he hath sent me.*

Declaring boldly and truthfully and lifting up his Father,
he's speaking not to keep the glory unto himself, but he is
speaking freely of the Father. He's given the Father the
honor for sending him to all mankind, even to those who
could not see, even to those whose eyes were blinded
because of their love for darkness. The word of God is so
good, and it is so true.

It's amazing, as we behold the children of men today, ones
that cannot differentiate between truth and error, between
righteousness and unrighteousness, between good and evil.
And it's because man loves darkness, according to St. John
3. Jesus said men love darkness rather than light because
their deeds are evil. But see, light will shine on the evil in
every heart, and that light will cause us to face the truth and
come unto our Maker and ask for forgiveness for the evil
that's in us.

But if we love to abide in darkness and do not want to see
that that is displeasing to God, we'll run from the light and
continue to abide in darkness because man would rather
have the darkness rather than Jesus, who is the light of the
world.

Whoever comes to Jesus must come as a sinner, knowing that we have need of God to deliver us. We cannot save ourselves. We cannot deliver ourselves from evil. Jesus came to deliver us from all evil. And this is the call of God today.

As it was when Jesus came, the Spirit of grace is still calling unto the children of men. Come ye out of darkness and put on light. Put on the Lord Jesus Christ.

Another writer wrote, quit ye like men and put on the Lord Jesus Christ. Quit like men? Yes, stop abiding in darkness. Stop walking in the path of destruction and come to life everlasting.

It's only in Jesus Christ, whom the Father has sent. And every word that proceedeth out of the mouth of Jesus was given to him of the Father. And this is why we must answer for what we have done to Jesus Christ, the love gift of God to humanity, to all humanity, regardless of nationality or color or creed.

Everyone must answer for what we have done with the light that God sent from heaven. Praise God in the highest. And it's up to us, precious ones, to choose where we want to abide.

Is it in the light or is it in darkness? Darkness is of the devil. We must understand that he was cast out of heaven and reserved in everlasting chains of darkness forever. And anyone that would do his deeds, Jesus Christ said, ye are of your father, the devil, for he was a liar from the beginning.

He created a lie. Everything that you hear contrary to the word of God is a lie. And Satan hates the truth. When he was in heaven as Lucifer, he rose up against God Almighty. And all the light that he shone, the rays of light, the Lord God took the light from him and cast him into outer darkness forever. And that is not what God has purposed for those who are of mankind.

He has chosen that we would walk in the light, that we would receive the light, and follow on in the light of the gospel that Jesus Christ preached. Praise God in the highest. So whether we be Jew or Gentile, God is telling us to believe on his only begotten son, that kings speak in that, that the Father gave unto him to speak. And that word that Jesus has spoken unto us is spirit, and it's life indeed.

Believe on the Lord Jesus Christ, accept him as your personal savior. He is the light of the world, and he will bring you into his marvelous light, and he will give you glorious understanding if you dare to believe on him, and he will lead you unto the Father. He will reveal the Father unto you by his Spirit. Glory to God in the highest. Believe his truth.

Darkness is covering the earth. In Isaiah the sixtieth chapter, the word of God says,

> *Arise, shine; for thy light is come, and the glory of the LORD is risen upon thee. For, behold, the darkness shall cover the earth, and gross darkness the people: but the LORD shall arise upon thee, and his glory shall be seen upon thee. And the Gentiles*

It is happening. When Jesus was born into this world, the kings of the east, hallelujah, saw that glorious light shining from afar, leading them to the light of God almighty, Jesus Christ. And that light from heaven led those kings to a humble little stable where Jesus, the Lord of heaven, the king of heaven, was born. Praise God in the highest.

Jesus, the love gift from God on high unto all humanity. Jesus, that precious light, that glorious light. And we see time is winding up, and men are abiding in gross darkness. Darkness has covered the earth, and gross darkness the people, because they refuse to see who Jesus is. He is not a mystery to those who believe on Him.

It is the will of God to reveal his Son, and it is the will of the Son to reveal the Father unto us, the children of men. We are the children of light when we believe on the Lord Jesus Christ.

Will you abide in the light? Will you come out of darkness? And those that are named in his name as Lord and Savior and friend, are you truly following him? Are you his disciple indeed? Are you continuing in his word, obedient to his word, walking as the Holy Spirit enlightens you? Take inventory of your heart.

Let's be honest before God, while there's yet time to be reconciled in wholeness and in fullness. Jesus is coming for his bride. He is coming for the church that he has already ordained to bring home to the Father.

Will you be part of that, that God Almighty sent Jesus to perform in the earth? We are his body. We are the members of his body. Worldwide, there are children of God that belong to the Father and to the Son and to the Holy Spirit.

Ask yourself, are you ready? Are you abiding truly in that, that the Holy Spirit has enlightened you to obey? If not, ask God's forgiveness and be reconciled unto him and come into the light and walk in the sweet fellowship and communion with your Father and with your Savior, Jesus Christ. The Holy Spirit will reveal them. It is the will of God that you know and understand who you are serving.

The height and the length and the breadth and the depth, and the width. The Lord wants you to know and understand who you are serving. Glory, Hallelujah.

You are fearfully and wonderfully made. You are not just flesh and blood. You are soul and spirit, and your soul longs to know its maker, to be in communion daily, constantly throughout the day with God, its creator.

So let not your mind alienate you, your complete being from knowing God, the creator. God wants you. He wants you.

The word of God says in Ephesians 4, verse 14,

> *that we henceforth be no more children, tossed to and fro, and carried about with every wind of doctrine, by the sleight of men, and cunning craftiness, whereby they lie in wait to deceive; but speaking the truth in love, may grow up into him in all things, which is the head, even Christ:*

Jesus is the head of this body worldwide. Jesus, the true Messiah, glory to his name. The Lord says, writing through Paul in the book of Ephesians,

> *from whom the whole body fitly joined together and compacted by that which every joint supplieth, according to the effectual working in the measure of every part, maketh increase of the body unto the edifying of itself in love.*

This is the will of God, worldwide, the children of God, fitly joined together and compacted by every joint, praise God, supplying, amen, every need of that body. As we look to the head, Jesus Christ, who is God's love and God's heartthrob. In verse 17, he says,

> *This I say therefore, and testify in the Lord, that ye henceforth walk not as other Gentiles walk, in the vanity of their mind, having the understanding darkened, being alienated from the life of God through the ignorance that is in them, because of the blindness of their heart: who being past feeling have given themselves over unto lasciviousness, to work all uncleanness with greediness.*

See, manifesting the works of the flesh when the heart is blinded from the truth. When you choose to walk in your own way, in the vanity of your own mind, it brings darkness.

But we are to walk in the mind of Christ, and the mind of Christ reveals the Father's will. It reveals the father's truth. It reveals the Father's desires unto the body of Jesus Christ.

So precious ones, walk in love, walk in the love of God, love him above everything else. Love him above yourself. Love him above your fellow men.

If you love God, if you put him first and desire to please only Him, you cannot help but love your fellow men. You cannot help but manifest the love of God unto your fellow men and to do right and justly by every man. But you must love God first.

You must love Him with all your heart, with all your soul, with all your mind. We're to walk in love. We're to put on the Lord Jesus Christ and walk in the light.

In Saint John 7, Jesus strove about, bringing forth the word of God to those who would not believe. They chose willfully not to believe, but to strive against the truth and to reject truth as they saw im. Don't let this be your way.

Put off the old way. Don't strive. No matter who you are, Jew or Gentile… choose Jesus.

Ask God the Father to reveal who Jesus is. God will open your understanding. He will bring you out of darkness into this glorious light. Let the glory of the Lord shine upon you. As Isaiah 60 says, let me read it again.

> *Arise, shine; for thy light is come, and the glory of the LORD is risen upon thee.*

Let his glory be risen upon you. Bring glory and honor to His name while you live and have your being. While you move about in this world, let the light of Jesus and the glory of his countenance be upon you. It is the will of God the Father. God so loved the world that He gave his only begotten Son that his glory might rest upon you and you might be a partaker of his divine nature.

Darkness is covering the earth and gross darkness the people, but come out of darkness and walk in this marvelous and glorious light, and God will give you good understanding to know his precious will.

God be with you till we meet again, amen.

Light vs. Darkness II

First Aired Dec 6th, 1998

Greetings, everyone. We thank God for this day that he hath made, and the Bible says, we shall rejoice and be glad in it. Surely God is good to us, all of us, all of humanity. God is good.

We thank the Lord for the word and the topic of the word, light versus darkness. We're living in a time, according to Isaiah, in the 60th chapter, that darkness has overtaken the minds of the people, and gross darkness is covering the earth.

God is light, and in Him there is no darkness, no, not at all. And those who are born again by the Spirit of God are children of light. Those who are not born again are called children of darkness.

Isaiah, the 60th chapter, tells us,

> *Arise, shine; for thy light is come, and the glory of the LORD is risen upon thee. For, behold, the darkness shall cover the earth, and gross darkness the people: but the LORD shall arise upon thee, and his glory shall be seen upon thee.*

Hallelujah. In Isaiah, the eighth chapter, beginning at the 16th verse,

> *Bind up the testimony, seal the law among my disciples. And I will wait upon the LORD, that*

In this hour, many are seeking for the powers of darkness.
They're seeking those who have contact with evil spirits.
It's gross…It is dark. Many are seeking for their fortunes to
be told and their history to be told unto them, for their
future to be told unto them from one that has a familiar
spirit, one that is in touch with the devil and his gifts of
divination. Demons revealing what they know and what
they've already done to humanity and calling themselves of
God's wisdom. It is not so.

Verse 19 again,

> *And when they shall say unto you, Seek unto them
> that have familiar spirits,*

People who are in touch with the dead,

> *and unto wizards that peep,*

People who have what they call that certain gift, but it's of
the devil, we're to only receive instructions from God
Almighty.

The answer is yes. God is still alive, and he is still on the
throne. You do not have to go after any other God, after
anyone with a familiar spirit, one that is familiar with the
devil and his works. You don't have to go after such a
person as that. And if you do, you must remember that God
is a jealous God and he made you for Himself.

He has given his spirit freely, he's poured out his spirit, his
spirit is here to guide us and lead us unto the true and living
God. We're not to go to that which is dead, and God has
reserved unto everlasting chains of darkness. We're to go to
God Almighty, he is alive.

This is what he's calling gross darkness. The enemy cannot
cast himself out. The devil cannot cast out a devil, lest his
house be divided, Jesus said.

It is time that we know who Jesus is. He is light, He is the
light of the world. And that light did not just become light
when he came to this earth; he is the light of heaven. Praise
his holy name. Verse 20,

> *To the law and to the testimony: if they speak not
> according to this word, it is because there is no light
> in them.*

We're to follow Jesus; if we go and follow anything else
contrary to the will of God, the Lord said there is no light in
them. And Jesus is coming soon. This is what it's all about.
This is what the preaching of the gospel is all about: to tell
you that Jesus is coming soon. It is later than we think.

Glory to God. There have been many false teachings and many false prophets saying false things. But anyone with any light at all will know, according to the scriptures and according to what we see happening in our day, in this present day in which we live. We know the scriptures, we know that Jesus is coming soon.

People are losing sight of what is right and what is wrong. They're not able to make a difference because of darkness, because of gross darkness. So this message is very timely, precious ones, we're to choose light. Jesus, is that light!

And the Holy Spirit will enlighten us unto Jesus Christ. His job, the Holy Spirit's job, is to teach us who Jesus is. To bring back his words to our remembrance as we read them and as we hear them taught, as we hear them preached, and enlighten us the more as to the meaning thereof.

That's the work of the Holy Spirit as we receive the truth. As we receive the truth, then the Holy Spirit will seal that word in us and make us shine the brighter with the light of the glorious gospel of Jesus Christ. Amen.

We do not need a witch or wizard to tell us lies. And if they tell you the truth, it's to bind you in a spirit of lies. It cannot bring deliverance to you. It's to bind you and blind you into darkness, everlasting darkness, because they are bound in chains and fetters. Let the Lord speak to your heart. Pray unto him.

Glory to His name. In Second Peter, chapter two, in verse 17, this is what God says, Oh God in the highest, show us the way, show us the way through your scriptures,

*These are wells without water, clouds that are
carried with a tempest; to whom the mist of
darkness is reserved for ever.*

People who will tell you to do different things or say it's
okay, everybody's doing it. Everybody is not doing it.

Who is he talking about? Verse 12 says,

*But these, as natural brute beasts, made to be taken
and destroyed, speak evil of the things that they
understand not; and shall utterly perish in their own
corruption;*

This is what we see today, man's own corruption…

*and shall receive the reward of
unrighteousness, as they that count it pleasure to
riot in the daytime. Spots they are and blemishes,
sporting themselves with their own deceivings while
they feast with you;*

They eat the word of God right along with you, right?
Come right in your midst. And yet they're there to bind you
to rob you, they're spots. The Bible says in verse 14,

*having eyes full of adultery, and that cannot cease
from sin; beguiling unstable souls: an heart they
have exercised with covetous practices; cursed
children:*

You see, God makes a difference between those that are his
and those who are not his. Everybody said we are all
children of God. No, we are all the creation of God.

But whoever we make our choice to serve, that's whose father's children we are. If we made our choice to serve God, if we've come unto him and received him and walk in the light of the gospel of Jesus Christ, then we are children of light with the children of the day. But if we choose to remain in darkness and go after those things that the flesh will do, then we are children of darkness, and our father is the devil.

It's our choice. And we can't say the devil made me do it. It's up to us to hear and receive Jesus Christ and walk in that precious light.

Jesus said, my father and your father, my God and your God. He's talking to those who have received him. That's what he came to do: to make us children of God, heirs of the kingdom of heaven and joint heirs with himself, Jesus Christ, joint heirs, making us joint heirs with him to inherit everything that heaven consists of. Glory to his name. What a mighty God we serve.

God did not intend for us to be cursed. He sent Jesus to deliver us from the curse of sin. But if we choose to abide in darkness and continue in our own way, we are under that curse… Cursed children.

This is the second Peter, the second chapter, verse 14. Verse 15,

> *which have forsaken the right way, and are gone astray, following the way of Balaam the son of Bosor, who loved the wages of unrighteousness;*

There are people that love darkness. They love sin, they love it. They're not just bound by it. They love to sin.

They don't want anything to do with the righteousness of God. And Balaam was that person. He was like that. He was gifted with knowledge and foresight, but he was also covetous and greedy.

God gave him to know that he could not curse that which God had blessed, although he tried because he was greedy. He wanted money, and he would lay down his own life to get it. He would lose out with God to get it. And Balaak, the king Balaak, told Balaam, if you just curse these people, curse them, I'll give you such and such reward. And God knows Balaam tried.

But God Almighty spoke to him, and he said, you cannot curse that which God has blessed. Today, men are trying to curse one another. But when God favors you, no one can curse you.

No matter what wizard they go to or witch to peep and to mutter, they cannot curse that which God has blessed. He says in verse 16,

> *but was rebuked.*

Balaam was rebuked,

> *but was rebuked for his iniquity: the dumb ass speaking with man's voice forbad the madness of the prophet.*

The madness of the prophet. It's a lot of mad prophets out here today. So,

They say this one has a spell over you, and this one has done you evil. The devil is evil, and his children are evil.

And the Lord has seen fit that we be here in this evil world, but redeemed, covered with the blood of Jesus Christ. And Peter asked, what harm can anyone do unto you if you be followers of that which is good? And we know there's only one good. That's God. Amen.

So why waste your time going to that which is evil to get blessed or to be lied to? Men can't bless you, and the devil can't bless you. Only God. Only God. Our blessings come from God. But if you go off to a false prophet seeking to be consoled and seeking to be told who's done this to you and who's done that back to you, you are abiding in darkness.

Read the story of King Manasseh, a most gross king of wickedness. He abode in darkness. And the Bible says he caused all Israel to sin because of his abominations.

Read the story of King Saul, how he sought to him a woman with a familiar spirit, one that could go and conjure up the dead. These things are an abomination in the eyes of God. And if you are called by his name, lose yourself from such an abomination if you're guilty.

Because you will pay the price in the end. Eternal separation from God if you don't come out from such gross darkness. God is light. And in him, there is no darkness. When I opened the word of God to speak unto you today, I did not have this on my heart. This is directly from God. He knows where each one of us lives. Praise his holy name. And it's time to put on the Lord Jesus Christ.

It's time to have no fellowship with the works of darkness. It's time to serve Jesus. And you don't have to be afraid of who's doing this to you, and who's doing that to you... No one can if you follow after that which is good.

And if you have been bound by the enemy, ask Jesus to set you free. He and he alone is that mighty deliverer. Don't run to false prophets and false teachers that will bind you even more so with their damnable lies. Glory to God in the highest.

If you want to serve Jesus, then you leave all of that behind you. Cast everything upon Jesus. He's already paid the price for your liberty. Praise his holy name. And he will deliver you. The Lord said through Peter,

> *These are wells without water, clouds that are carried with a tempest; to whom the mist of darkness is reserved for ever.*

They have no right to the tree of life, nor the light of that glorious city that we shall abide in. They are reserved unto everlasting darkness.

> *For when they speak great swelling words of vanity,*

That means lying to you.

> *they allure through the lusts of the flesh, through much wantonness, those that were clean escaped from them who live in error.*

And that's what God is calling us into, cleanness, better called, holiness. Praise his holy name.

> *those that were clean escaped from them who live in error. While they promise them liberty, they themselves are the servants of corruption:*

They can't deliver you; only Jesus can.

> *for of whom a man is overcome, of the same is he brought in bondage. For if after they have escaped the pollutions of the world through the knowledge of the Lord and Saviour Jesus Christ, they are again entangled therein, and overcome, the latter end is worse with them than the beginning.*

It's time to walk in the light. Colossians, the first chapter in the 12th verse tells us,

> *giving thanks unto the Father, which hath made us meet to be partakers of the inheritance of the saints in light*

Jesus, the light of the world. As I said before, Jesus came to make us joint heirs with him in the kingdom of his Father God. Verse 13 says,

> *who hath delivered us from the power of darkness, and hath translated us into the kingdom of his dear Son: in whom we have redemption through his blood, even the forgiveness of sins:*

Jesus, is that light! And he hath delivered us that are born again from the power of darkness. So don't entangle yourselves again with such wickedness.

So much corruption is going on in the world today. And so many people are running after wizards and witches. There's been a great revival of witches and their evil works.

Glory to Jesus. Gross darkness has overtaken their minds. And no child of God has the right to seek after such a mess as that. It's gross darkness! And they won't stop on a network. They'll come into your church.

They'll come right after you to deceive you, to bind you. But you that are clean, you that have escaped them, stay clean. Stay clean. Jesus Christ has redeemed you with his blood.

Praise God. The word of God is right. And the word of God is righteous, altogether. The Lord is that light. Praise his holy name. The first chapter of John. Let's read.

> *In the beginning was the Word, and the Word was with God, and the Word was God. The same was in the beginning with God. All things were made by him; and without him was not any thing made that was made. In him was life; and the life was the light of men.*

If you want to walk in the light, you must receive the life of Jesus Christ.

> *And the light shineth in darkness; and the darkness comprehended it not.*

When Jesus came shining brightly, the world was so full of darkness that they did not know, nor understand, nor did they believe in the Lord Jesus Christ.

So,

> *There was a man sent from God, whose name was John. The same came for a witness, to bear witness of the Light, that all men through him might believe.*

Not through John, but Jesus, the light. He is speaking of himself.

> *He was not that Light, but was sent to bear witness of that Light.*

And John bore witness. He said, there comes one mightier than I. Glory to Jesus.

> That was the true Light, which lighteth every man that cometh into the world.

Jesus, is that light! We're soon to celebrate the birth of Jesus Christ, and man, so full of darkness, they heap unto themselves how they're going to have a good time during the Christmas holidays. They'll go off buying gifts, only because they feel that it's the time to give. But see, if they knew the true light, they would know and accept Jesus Christ as that light from heaven. And they would not give just at the time of Christmas. Their life would be full of giving every day of the year. Praise God.

And it would not be selfish giving. Not giving to receive. But giving because of the love and the light of Jesus Christ.

And that's year-round. Because there are people all over the world that needs our gifts of love. They need our attention.

Jesus,

That was the true Light, which lighteth every man that cometh into the world. He was in the world, and the world was made by him, and the world knew him not. He came unto his own, and his own received him not. But as many as received him, to them gave he power to become the sons of God,

He gave power to be delivered from Satan's darkness. It takes the power of Jesus Christ. And whosoever desires to come unto him. He will give you the power to be liberated from Satan. To come from his dominion of darkness. Into the marvelous light of the glorious gospel, and to live thereby in Jesus every day.

But as many as received him, to them gave he power to become the sons of God, even to them that believe on his name:

That's how powerful his name is, Jesus, glory to his name. God gave Jesus that name. For it means he shall save his people from their sins. That's why the name Jesus is given. It means salvation. You want to celebrate Christmas? Give thanks unto God that sent Jesus Christ. Amen.

For he is that light. And he's waiting for you to surrender. That he might shine in your life eternal.

God be with you. Amen and amen. Amen.

God Will Cast Satan Into Hell

God is just, and he's pure, he's holy, and he will not accept anything less. We have to keep this in mind. God will not accept anything less than what he has required. This is why hell has enlarged its mouth.

There have been too many reports of people going, passing from this life to the other, and God allowing them to come back. All is not true. Some are totally demonic, but some… are true. And He's allowing this to be that we might escape ourselves and the devil and hellfire.

Father, in the powerful name of Jesus, we're asking you to take charge of your word. I yield to the Holy Spirit, leaning upon you, Father, for nothing do I know of myself. Send your word with fire. Let it burn the wood, the hay, and stubble now.

Bring clarity to every confused mind. Bring down every opponent who would rebel against you. We loose your authority and your power to work in our hearts and in our minds and send forth the spirit of revelation and understanding that we might know and understand what you have written here, that we might be knowledgeable and powerful, that we might be equipped with the truth rightly divided with an understanding heart as we witness and lift up the name of thy Son, Jesus, that we might know what is yet to come by thy Spirit.

For you have said, Lord Jesus, the Holy Ghost will show us things to come. Show us today. Anoint our eyes that we might see and our ears that we might hear, and sober our hearts and help us to be about your business. We ask in Jesus' name, and I cast out the enemy, that old liar, that old deceiver. I bind you, and I cast you out. In Jesus' authoritative name, amen and amen.

Ezekiel 28,

> *The word of the LORD came again unto me, saying, Son of man, say unto the prince of Tyrus, Thus saith the Lord GOD; Because thine heart is lifted up, and thou hast said, I am a God, I sit in the seat of God, in the midst of the seas; yet thou art a man, and not God, though thou set thine heart as the heart of God: behold, thou art wiser than Daniel; there is no secret that they can hide from thee: with thy wisdom and with thine understanding thou hast gotten thee riches, and hast gotten gold and silver into thy treasures:*
>
> *By thy great wisdom and by thy traffic hast thou increased thy riches and thine heart is lifted up because of thy riches. Therefore thus saith the Lord, God, because thou hast set thine heart as the heart of God, behold, therefore I will bring strangers upon thee, the terrible of the nations, and they shall draw their swords against the beauty of thy wisdom and they shall defile thy brightness.*
>
> *They shall bring thee down to the pit, and thou shalt die the deaths of them that are slain in the midst of the seas. Wilt thou yet say before him that slayeth thee, I am God? but thou shalt be a man, and no*

God, in the hand of him that slayeth thee. Thou shalt die the deaths of the uncircumcised by the hand of strangers: for I have spoken it, saith the Lord GOD.

Moreover the word of the LORD came unto me, saying, Son of man, take up a lamentation upon the king of Tyrus, and say unto him, Thus saith the Lord GOD; Thou sealest up the sum, full of wisdom, and perfect in beauty. Thou hast been in Eden the garden of God; every precious stone was thy covering, the sardius, topaz, and the diamond, the beryl, the onyx, and the jasper, the sapphire, the emerald, and the carbuncle, and gold: the workmanship of thy tabrets and of thy pipes was prepared in thee in the day that thou wast created.

Thou art the anointed cherub that covereth; and I have set thee so: thou wast upon the holy mountain of God; thou hast walked up and down in the midst of the stones of fire. Thou wast perfect in thy ways from the day that thou wast created, till iniquity was found in thee. By the multitude of thy merchandise they have filled the midst of thee with violence, and thou hast sinned:

therefore I will cast thee as profane out of the mountain of God: and I will destroy thee, O covering cherub, from the midst of the stones of fire. Thine heart was lifted up because of thy beauty, thou hast corrupted thy wisdom by reason of thy brightness: I will cast thee to the ground, I will lay thee before kings, that they may behold thee. Thou hast defiled thy sanctuaries by the multitude of thine iniquities, by the iniquity of thy traffick;

therefore will I bring forth a fire from the midst of thee, it shall devour thee, and I will bring thee to ashes upon the earth in the sight of all them that behold thee. All they that know thee among the people shall be astonished at thee: thou shalt be a terror, and never shalt thou be any more.

Again the word of the LORD came unto me, saying, Son of man, set thy face against Zidon, and prophesy against it, and say, Thus saith the Lord GOD; Behold, I am against thee, O Zidon; and I will be glorified in the midst of thee: and they shall know that I am the LORD, when I shall have executed judgments in her, and shall be sanctified in her. For I will send into her pestilence, and blood into her streets; and the wounded shall be judged in the midst of her by the sword upon her on every side; and they shall know that I am the LORD.

And there shall be no more a pricking brier unto the house of Israel, nor any grieving thorn of all that are round about them, that despised them; and they shall know that I am the Lord GOD.

Thus saith the Lord GOD; When I shall have gathered the house of Israel from the people among whom they are scattered, and shall be sanctified in them in the sight of the heathen, then shall they dwell in their land that I have given to my servant Jacob. And they shall dwell safely therein, and shall

*build houses, and plant vineyards; yea, they shall
dwell with confidence, when I have executed
judgments upon all those that despise them round
about them; and they shall know that
I am the LORD their God.*

Ezekiel chapter 28 in the fullness. Isaiah 14,

*For the LORD will have mercy on Jacob, and will
yet choose Israel, and set them in their own land:
and the strangers shall be joined with them, and
they shall cleave to the house of Jacob.*

Not Allah or Mohammed, but Jacob.

*And the people shall take them, and bring them to
their place: and the house of Israel shall possess
them in the land of the LORD for servants and
handmaids: and they shall take them captives,
whose captives they were; and they shall rule over
their oppressors.*

*And it shall come to pass in the day that
the LORD shall give thee rest from thy sorrow, and
from thy fear, and from the hard bondage wherein
thou wast made to serve, that thou shalt take up this
proverb against the king of Babylon, and say, How
hath the oppressor ceased! the golden city
ceased! The LORD hath broken the staff of the
wicked, and the sceptre of the rulers. He who smote
the people in wrath with a continual stroke, he that
ruled the nations in anger, is persecuted, and none
hindereth.*

So you see, in Ezekiel 28, when God says, King of Tyrus,
he is speaking of the devil. God would say he would be just

like a man, and that's why he called him man. And Isaiah speaks even more clearly through the anointing of God.

He makes it very clear. Verse 16,

> *They that see thee shall narrowly look upon*
> *thee, and consider thee, saying, Is this the man*

And he makes it very clear that he is speaking of Lucifer. If you check verse 12,

> *How art thou fallen from heaven, O Lucifer, son of*
> *the morning!*

But his name is no longer Lucifer, because he's a fallen devil. He's called the dragon, that old serpent, that great deceiver, the wicked one, satan, the destroyer, the liar. And he's got a list of names. It's too numerous to name right now. Verse 17,

> *That made the world as a wilderness, and destroyed*
> *the cities thereof; that opened not the house of his*
> *prisoners?*

He gets his iron-clad fist wrapped around your heart and around your mind. He binds, and he will not let go. That's why a greater power than his must break the yoke. And that power is Jesus. He's not only the wisdom of God, He's the power of God!

That's why I glory in Jesus. Because satan is a robber. He's a hard taskmaster. He binds and will not let go. And this is why we dare not fear him. Many saints won't even mention his name, because they fear his retaliation.

But we have more power of Jesus Christ in one little fingernail than all of Satan's kingdom and all of his imps. If we would only be still enough to seek God's face and let God reveal unto us who we have become in Christ Jesus because of Jesus.

Too many Christians are forfeiting their rights as children of God. And running off to the arms of the flesh. Seeking counsel, seeking help. Seeking a way out. When all they've got to do is see who Jesus is. And know that they are standing in the power of Jesus. And are able to thwart any war that comes against us.

For God Jehovah says we are his battle axe and weapons of war. And we're not to give the devil any glory. Nor any of his servants. We're to fear no man. And if God calls him a man, then we don't fear him. Glory to God in the highest.

God dares us to fear man. He said, what is man that thou art fearful of, a man that shall die? And God has declared here that he shall be ashes, he shall die.

There is a consuming fire coming. Glory be to God, and satan shall die. We're not talking about the thousand years when he's going to be bound. He is going to die! Jesus, the almighty conquering king, will see to it that Satan shall die! He's going to die. You'd be stupid enough to serve him if you want to. But bless God, we're on the winning side.

Jesus! God's Almighty Conqueror!

And this same Jesus has made us more than conquerors. Because he loves us. He loves us and has imparted that same power unto us. And we're not forsaken, he's in us, and we're in him. Glory be to God, and not for one fleeting moment will we forget who Jesus is. And not for one moment will we forget who the enemy is.

The only way we shall remain victorious is… we've got to see who the devil is. And we have got to allow Jesus Christ to show us the enemy's strategies. Only Christ knows where he is. He goes to and fro, up and down in the earth. Performing his wickedness and destroying nations and destroying souls. Setting up kings of nations. And presidents.

And we got to stay with the mind of Christ. To know where our enemy is. And bless God by faith in Jesus name, we have to dislodge him. Because see, we have to stay here until God is ready for us to come home. And bless God, we're not going to stay here miserable.

Because Jesus is peace, not in this world. He did not pray for the peace of this world. But for all that the Father God has given him. He said my peace I give unto you. When Jesus prayed in the 17th chapter of Saint John, he said I do not pray for the world. But for them that thou hast given me. Glory to God in the highest.

We want to run around and lovey-dovey everybody, everybody. Every demon, every demon possessed. No, no, no, no, no. Jesus is yet seeking to save that which is lost. But we'd better give him God's just Word.

God loves you. You'd better tell them that there's a burning hell. I will never forget when I was on my way to Africa for the first time. God told me that many of my ministers have failed me. How Lord? They tell the people of my love. And of my heaven. But they fail to warn the people of a burning hell.

He said many of his ministers, and I was one of them. Didn't want to touch it. Unpleasant. Didn't even want to think about it. Oh God, just help me to get these souls from him. But that's partially done. Some people are so hard-hearted... Christians even. So tough and so full of deception, so full of self and hell… You'd better tell them where they're going!

Or we'll never get into those gates either. Because their blood, the hands will be so sticky with the blood of those that we fail to warn, that God will not want any parts of us either. You see, it's going to be to the Christians that He's going to say, "Depart from me, I never knew you."

We'd better be sober. We have to understand that every word that's written here shall come to pass. Somebody will be hearing these negative words. Depart from me, I never knew you.

To those who never accepted Christ as their personal Savior, never owned him. They won't have a chance to get to those pearly gates. All He will say to them is depart, depart… depart.

But to those who professed his name and said that they were his. Lord have not we done many wonderful works in your name? We testified to others. You mean you're going to send me to hell?

I never knew you… I never knew you. So you see why God has given us the opportunity to get to know him like the apostle Paul.

No matter how close Paul lived with Jesus Christ. His aim, his goal ultimately was… "Oh, to know him!" And that has to be our heartbeat daily.

Not, oh Lord, I'm your precious jewel. But oh God, I want more of you. Draw me closer. And then bless God, get down to business. And be drawn closer. Hallelujah. This is serious. And sobering. God's not playing.

And he's not going to alter his word just because he made us. He didn't alter his word when his only begotten Son was in the garden praying that that cup of death would pass from him. Jesus had to succumb to the will of God. To bring the ultimate glory. And we too, must succumb to what is written here. Pride cometh before destruction.

Haughtiness, rebellion… We talk about how grossly wicked witchcraft is. Be stubborn and rebellious, God puts it on the same level, same level. We've got to clean up. We have to see ourselves as God sees us. And many of us don't want that. That's why you don't want to seek Him.

Pray our little prayers, read a couple of verses... gone! You say, "Thank you for the blood. I'm yours, Lord, I'm yours."

The Lord is saying, are you? And has to say it after us. Because our backs are going the other way. It's time to take inventory.

Don't you know God created Lucifer for his glory? And God set him above all the angels in Heaven. God made him the son of the morning. He was over music, he was the brightness, and the brightest cherub. Beautiful!

What I'm really saying here and what God is saying. Is that what he created, God loved… He loved Lucifer. He gloried in Lucifer. So much so that he gave him his brightness. And made him most beautiful than all the other angels. Perfected him with wisdom and knowledge. Great abilities! The highest in rank of all the angelic host. Until sin was found in him!

When he rose up to overthrow God. He said, "I will be as the most high." And you know where God stationed him? In the holy mountain on the side of the north. See how we sing that song? That's where he was. And there was no repentance in him. Because he went about gathering more to his wicked thoughts.

And deceived a third part of God's created angelic host, which are demons now, in their fallen, blackened state. That's who Lucifer has become. And his sole purpose is to get back at God by overthrowing souls, by destroying souls, by deceiving souls that God loves.

Satan is judged; he will not be judged anymore; he'll just be fought and cast to the pit. But we yet have to approach the judgment seat of Christ. So we better take heed how we listen to the devil. We better find out who he really is. And keep him fleeing. The only way we can make Satan flee.

Is to submit ourselves to God on a continual basis. This is no one-time affair; we have to give ourselves daily unto God. Amen. Yesterday was only for yesterday.

Now, when we come unto Him, it should be with a lifetime commitment. But many things come against us.

And we have to make decisions, gross decisions, and sometimes small decisions. However…we must ever keep in our minds. That we are yielding our members unto God. We have an enemy that is not called Satan only, but self. And that's the one Jesus said. Deny yourselves, take up your cross, and follow me.

And if we don't know who self is, we'd better run to Jesus. Ask him to reveal that honorary thing in us. For self is nothing beautiful. There is no beauty in the old man. Paul says reckon him dead, reckon yourselves dead. That's how great an enemy self is to God, and to our souls. Hallelujah. Let's proceed.

Isaiah 14, verse 18,

> *All the kings of the nations, even all of them, lie in glory, every one in his own house. But thou art cast out of thy grave like an abominable branch, and as the raiment of those that are slain, thrust through with a sword, that go down to the stones of the pit; as a carcase trodden under feet.*
>
> *Thou shalt not be joined with them in burial, because thou hast destroyed thy land, and slain thy*

*people: the seed of evildoers shall never be
renowned. Prepare slaughter for his children*

 See, not only for him, and his demons, prepare slaughter
for his children.

*Thou shalt not be joined with them in burial,
because thou hast destroyed thy land, and slain thy
people: the seed of evildoers shall never be
renowned. Prepare slaughter for his children*

 God's gonna cleanse this world. Amen. He's gonna destroy
every abomination, every filthy place, and every filthy
person. It's going to happen because God is holy in nature.
Christian, God is holy. And this world… He will not bring
the kingdom of heaven into this world until it's cleansed.

It shall be a new heaven. And a new earth, He's gonna
purify, He's gonna burn and consume. That's the way he's
going to purify. Just like he sanctifies us, consecrates our
lives… It's through the furnace. That's where he brings us.
We may go into the furnace kicking and hauling and
squirreling. But God knows the canker that's in us. And
God is after gold. And God is after silver.

Away with the hay and stubble and wood. God wants gold!
And pure gold is tried in the fire! And we'd rather go
through God's purging fires now, than his consuming fire,
later! Amen. It's time to sober up. Amen.

Glory be to God. I do not feel sorry for any Christian who
says they are struggling, struggling, trying to make a
decision. Whether they're gonna serve God or not… Just
get out of my way! I don't have time for that foolishness. I

just clamp my mouth and listen. Because it's foolish! To even contemplate such a thing!

When God is so loving and merciful and long-suffering. And you still can't make up your mind whether you're gonna be holy or not? But you know what the problem is? They're afraid of sin being found out. But God already knows. He knows what we're guilty of. We can't run from Him! He knows!

And bless God those that's walking with Him knows too. Oh yes, the Holy Ghost, He's a squealer.. He does, He reveals the intents of men's hearts…He does! None of us know any heart but the Holy Ghost in us. Remember when Jesus would be amongst the scribes and the Pharisees? And the Holy Ghost would give Jesus to perceive what was in their hearts. That's the same Holy Ghost. Only one… Only one.

And He's vast and wide and big and deep enough to be in us all. Praise God in the highest! So just come out from the deception, come out from being a follower of Lucifer. Lucifer, see, was still Lucifer while he was yet being a deceiver. And that's the way some so-called Christians are trying to follow God, as Lucifer, a deceiver.

God is genuine; He's just. This is one thing that we found in the study of Philippians 4:8. Honest! Whatsoever things are honest. And we found that honest means straightforward. Glory be to God. The heart is open, pure, and honest.

And didn't Jesus say that the seed that fell on good ground was the honest ground? The honest ground. Time to be honest now. Just stop your lying. You can tell the biggest lie just by keeping your mouth shut and doing. And God is saying stop it. You're deceiving only yourself. Even the devil has run off from you. Glory to God in the highest. Left you standing alone as a fool. Amen.

Sometimes I just shake my head. Lord, how big a fool do they think I am? To clap those lips together. And move that tongue and tell me those lies…Stupid! As if I'm not praying. As if I'm not walking with God. As if the Lord does not love me. And as if the Lord has a covering over my eyes. The devil is a liar!

Glory to God. My eyes are open! I told you I've got to live where God can hear me. So my eyes have got to be open. And we all better live that way. Because God forbids us to be ignorant concerning the devil's devices. You think Jesus would just stand up there saying, a quotation, the devil is a liar. No! No! He wants us to know that the devil IS a liar! Glory to God in the highest.

And the father of lies, he invented them. Glory to God in the highest! Why would you be his priestess? Why would you be his witch? Why would you be his imp? Why would you be his wizard? Why? When he's a defeated fool.

Christ has already stripped him. Jesus came to destroy the works of the devil. In the eyes of God, he's destroyed! In the eyes of those who serve God, he is destroyed already! That's what faith is all about!

That's why we take courage. That's why we stand against him, though he spews out his venom against us. We don't fear him. Glory to God in the highest. We are on God's side.

And more than that, God is on our side. Praise God. So we can help but win! Hallelujah.

Do it God's way. Cause this is the fate of those who hate God. I tried my best to get to you to build you up, but the Lord… I stood up here, and I started, but the Lord said no, you give them what I gave you. Glory to God in the highest. Cause God knows our hearts!

And he knows what we need to hear. And you in radio land. God knows who you are. Stop your devilish works of iniquity! Repent of your ways and turn! And call on the name of Jesus. And let him deliver you. Hallelujah. This God you shall meet. You shall surely meet him. Verse 21,

> *Prepare slaughter for his children for the iniquity of their fathers; that they do not rise, nor possess the land,*

I heard you singing. "Rise up, ye strong, possess the land." We shall possess the land, the whole land, the entire land. And all nations we shall possess, when God brings his kingdom with the saints to this earth. The meek shall inherit the earth. But it's future tense, even now it's future tense. There is much more wickedness that has to be performed according to the prophecies of God.

And I'll show you in the book of Revelation. The Lord says.

> *For I will rise up against them, saith the LORD of hosts, and cut off from Babylon the name, and remnant, and son, and nephew, saith the LORD. I will also make it a possession for the bittern, and*

You can't pray it down; God has already spoken, He
purposed it, and it shall come to pass. Glory to God. It's
going to be.

Who has the power? Who has the wisdom? Who has the
authority? To disannul what God has said. No one! And
keep in mind satan is a man. Glory to God!

When God stretches his hand out to war...There is no hand,
no purpose, no mind, no power, that can break God's hand.
Glory hallelujah. Hallelujah. Revelations 19,

*glory, and honour, and power, unto the Lord our
God: for true and righteous are his judgments:*

You see? True and righteous are his judgments. Whatever
he does it's right. He shall never be unjust or unfair.

> *for he hath judged the great whore, which did
> corrupt the earth with her fornication, and hath
> avenged the blood of his servants at her hand. And
> again they said, Alleluia.*

> *And her smoke rose up for ever and ever. And the
> four and twenty elders and the four beasts fell down
> and worshipped God that sat on the throne, saying,
> Amen; Alleluia. And a voice came out of the throne,
> saying, Praise our God, all ye his servants, and ye
> that fear him, both small and great.*

> *And I heard as it were the voice of a great
> multitude, and as the voice of many waters, and as
> the voice of mighty thunderings, saying, Alleluia:
> for the Lord God omnipotent reigneth. Let us be
> glad and rejoice, and give honour to him: for the
> marriage of the Lamb is come, and his wife hath
> made herself ready.*

She has done it! She has done it! His wife…that's us. Glory
be to God. Hath made herself… By obeying the word of
God! By seeking his beauty, by being clothed in his
majesty, and his glory! By supping with him, eating him,
drinking him. Praise God in the highest! Doing his
commandments! Making herself ready continuously!

Praise God! Keeping herself washed in the blood of Jesus!

Glory to God in the highest.

For his wife hath made herself ready.

Glory to God in the highest! Beautiful! Beautified with the presence of Jesus Christ. Made herself ready, just and pure, righteous altogether. The wife, or the bride of Jesus Christ. Hallelujah. We've got to obey. We've got to put on Jesus. We've got to put him on. We've got to be pure and true. And honest and just. We have to report the good things of God. Amen and amen!

We must be righteous. Praise God in our living. Glory to God. We saints, and especially we women, but all saints. Men and women, children alike. Must adorn ourselves in godly array! Praise God. Not exposed in our bodies to the world! Glory to his name.

God is holy! And saints, we must be holy! You might think it's from the old school. But this God I serve is ancient! Praise God in the highest. If you want to be beautiful. Adorn yourself! Make yourself beautiful in God's sight. And not as the world thinks, but as the holy spirit dictates to us.

Have you ever gone shopping and God says don't you get that, you won't look proper in this. Well, if he hasn't, bless God you're not listening. You're not listening! It's time to get sanctified from this world. Amen. It's time to consecrate your lives unto Him, most high! Glory to God in the highest. Hallelujah.

I've got to preach it as it is. Love me or leave me, it's all right! But bless God, this God you'll meet. Amen, and the same gospel, you shall hear. Glory be to God. It'll save you! Or destroy you! It's time to clean up Zion. Hallelujah. My Lord and my God! Time to wake up, Zion!

Wake up! Wake up! Time for the saints to blow the trumpet as never before! Glory to God in the highest. Bless his holy name. He's going to adorn us. In his beautiful robe of righteousness. Finally. Amen.

But saints. We must have that robe. Of righteousness on us now. We're going to have a change of arraignment. This mortal body needs clothing. Amen. But this spiritual being, this glorified body, will be clothed with the robe of righteousness. Amen. That we have earned down here.

Do you hear me? The works we do is going to weigh out how we are going to be in the end. Hallelujah. I'm talking about the works of righteousness. Hallelujah. Obey him!

The Holy Spirit is at work sanctifying the church; don't rebel. Don't be like a witch. Amen. Humble yourself, break before him. It's time to break. Break off your fallow ground! God's going to remove the thorns and the briars. Glory to God. Hallelujah. Amen.

You bite and kick, that's thorns and briars. God said he'll remove you, He's going to burn you, Amen, Away! Ezekiel 28. You read it, go back and read it. Hallelujah. And every time I say it. It is not me, it's God! Telling you to get the word of God in you. Read it!

Read it!! And tremble at his word! You stop sitting stout-hearted and stubborn, (saying within yourself) "Who does she think she is?"

I'm a servant of the most high God. And I speak only that, that He put in this mouth! Hallelujah. Because I've got to answer to Him, I see no flesh, no blood, no friends, not even foes. I see what God says, the more he pumps me, the more it's coming out! Hallelujah.

Because I want to lie down in peace, and I want to rise up with the same confidence that my God hears me when I pray. Glory to his name!

Get your eyes off this world. Get your eyes on Jesus. He's not the prince of this world, so get your eyes on Jesus. He's the Prince of Peace. Coming out from heaven. He's coming for us. Praise his holy name. Praise his holy name. Hallelujah. I'm gonna read six again,

> *And I heard as it were the voice of a great multitude, and as the voice of many waters, and as the voice of mighty thunderings, saying, Alleluia: for the Lord God omnipotent reigneth.*

He is the Lord God omnipotent, and he reigns. Not Lucifer, not satan, not that old destroyer…Jesus, He reigns.

> *Let us be glad and rejoice, and give honour to him:*

That's the state of being God wants us in. And saints it can't be, when we are not in agreement with Him. We have to be in agreement with what he says. Embrace what he says. Because he's right.

He can't lie. And what he says is for our good, it's for our good. And he is not appealing to our self-life, He is talking to that which is truly within. Our innermost being, that's who he's talking to. And this is why the spirit of God says he that hath an ear. If you're truly alive unto him, let him hear what the spirit saith unto the churches, praise God. In verse 8,

> *And to her was granted that she should be arrayed in fine linen*

See, it's in the future tense, but we're preparing for it now. Our clothing, our wardrobe…

> *And to her was granted that she should be arrayed in fine linen, clean and white: for the fine linen is the righteousness of saints.*

Do what's right. When God speaks to your heart. You know, Jesus, as I was preparing this morning. He brought to my remembrance… I was thinking about the stubbornness of some here, and how they despise, how they despise the counsel of the Lord.

Jesus brought these words back to me. When he told certain people. If you do not believe me, believe for the very works' sake. And what he was saying to me is, even though you don't believe what this handmaiden of God is saying. Believe his word. Because I'm telling you what's written here. I'm not making anything up. I'm trembling and fearing.

I know I gotta stand before Him like everybody else. So I'm in your same state. I gotta hear just like you, He's using this vessel. But I've gotta obey just like you. Just like you, He's requiring of me. Just because he's using me doesn't make me exempt. I must be obedient just like you.

And I'm running for my life. Glory to God in the highest. Not because, or only because I want to escape hell, but I want to be with Jesus. I want to go home. Glory to his name. Verse 9,

> *And he saith unto me, Write, Blessed are they which are called unto the marriage supper of the Lamb. And he saith unto me, These are the true sayings of God.*

So are you going to be blessed? Are you of that blessed group?

> *Blessed are they which are called unto the marriage supper*

We get invitations. And we may say, no, no, I don't think I want to come. But are you going to say that to him? We're going to sit down at the marriage supper. Angels will be serving us. Glory to God in the highest. The redeemed of the earth. We're going in, Amen. The marriage supper. You know, after a marriage, don't we have a reception?

The reception…the angels will be receiving us. God the Father will be receiving us. We're going to sit down and have a great reception. The marriage supper it's called. Because we made it in. Hallelujah. His wife hath made herself ready.

*And I fell at his feet to worship him. And he said
unto me, See thou do it not: I am thy fellowservant,*

This is an angel talking to John.

and of thy brethren that have the testimony of Jesus:

He's gone on and received his reward of an angel.

*worship God: for the testimony of Jesus is the spirit
of prophecy.*

The testimony of Jesus is the spirit of prophecy…It is the
spirit of prophecy. What Jesus says is prophecy. It's the
spirit of prophecy. It's coming to pass. He is not a false
prophet. Praise God.

This is why he says, these are the true sayings of God.

*And I saw heaven opened, and behold a white
horse; and he that sat upon him was called Faithful
and True,*

Here he is again.

and in righteousness he doth judge and make war.

You think He's not? We call him the Lamb of God now, but
he's going to be the Lion of Judah. A warmonger. Amen.
He's going to annihilate his enemies. He's going to
overthrow and in righteousness He's not going to make any
mistakes, nor accuse anybody falsely, glory to God,
because he's faithful and true!

and in righteousness he doth judge

And when he judges what he sees, He's going to declare war.

His eyes were as a flame of fire, and on his head were many crowns;

Many, one head.

> *and he had a name written, that no man knew, but he himself.*

All of this is for purpose.

> *And he was clothed with a vesture dipped in blood:*

In blood.

> *and his name is called The Word of God.*

The Word, capitalized, the Living Word. The Word of God. Look at him, look at him anew. Look at him in a greater dimension here. Hallelujah. Ask God to widen the capacity of your heart. To receive this Christ. Hallelujah. Not just the man, the Son of Man. But God!

> *And the armies which were in heaven*

The armies, plural, different ranks.

> *the armies which were in heaven followed him upon white horses, clothed in fine linen,*

That's the saints.

> *white and clean. And out of his mouth goeth a sharp sword, that with it he should smite the nations:*

The word of his mouth, out of his mouth!

Well, that same God spoke the world into existence with his mouth. So it's no marvel that out of his mouth he's gonna smite the wicked.

> *and he shall rule them with a rod of iron: and he treadeth the winepress of the fierceness and wrath of Almighty God. And he hath on his vesture and on his thigh a name written, KING OF KINGS, AND Lord OF LORDS.*

> *And I saw an angel standing in the sun;*

An angel standing in the sun. We're human beings, the sun is millions of miles away, and we can't even stand to be in the sun in the heat of the day. We're looking for shelter. Amen, to protect us from the sun's rays. And here's an angel standing in the sun! Oh, what a mighty God!

> *And I saw an angel standing in the sun; and he cried with a loud voice, saying to all the fowls that fly in the midst of heaven, Come and gather yourselves together unto the supper of the great God;*

And that's not of the bride. This is the supper of the slaughter of the wrath of God.

> *that ye may eat the flesh of kings, and the flesh of captains, and the flesh of mighty men, and the flesh of horses, and of them that sit on them, and the flesh of all men, both free and bond, both small and great.*

And that includes the rich and the poor alike.

*And I saw the beast, and the kings of the earth, and
their armies,*

Isn't this foolish?

*gathered together to make war against him that sat
on the horse, and against his army.*

Insanity!

*And the beast was taken, and with him the false
prophet that wrought miracles before him, with
which he deceived them that had received the mark
of the beast, and them that worshipped his image.
These both were cast alive into a lake of fire
burning with brimstone. And the remnant were slain
with the sword of him that sat upon the horse,
which sword proceeded out of his mouth: and all
the fowls were filled with their flesh.*

*And I saw an angel come down from heaven, having
the key of the bottomless pit and a great chain in his
hand.*

One angel… one.

*And he laid hold on the dragon, that old serpent,
which is the Devil, and Satan, and bound him a
thousand years,*

One angel… one.

Now that's how puny Satan is, right now. Glory to God in
the highest!

God's two-third angelic host. And only one, one angel comes down from heaven with a great chain and lay hold on that old serpent, that old dragon, that old devil. that old Satan… and binds him! Hallelujah.

And God says, behold I give you power over all devils! It's time to wake up! It's time to realize who we are! Amen. God sends one angel.

And he tells us human beings, His disciples, His followers,

"Behold, I give you power over all devils."

And I believe it! I believe it! That's why I'm a warmonger today. Glory be to God. That's why I don't fear him. Because I believe my God. I believe that that's why I'm filled with the Holy Ghost. I believe that's why He empowers me day by day. Amen.

That not only do I live holy, and not only do I have the strength and power to declare His word, but that I would stand against my foes! Glory be to God. And execute the judgments written! For my righteousness is of God!

Our righteousness is of God, saith the Lord of hosts. We got to know who we are, what Christ has made us to be. Follow Him, hate sin, run from the evil, cling to that which is acceptable and good in the eyes of God. Stay with him, He's the Word, He's the living Word. He can't fail us. Glory be to God.

He's come this way as the Son of man, so he knows exactly what goes on inside of us human beings. He knows the temptations that come against us. He knows the wicked imagination of this world. Amen. That satan would entice us with. But he commands us to take the shield of faith and the sword of the Spirit. Put on the whole armor of God that we might be able to quench those fiery darts. Glory be to God.

Don't come crying to me if you don't want to overcome. Don't come crying to me, don't. Don't try to lay your guilt on me. I'm one of those five wise virgins! You go and buy for yourself.

Glory to God in the highest. Don't give me that gibberish. Praise God. Trying to make me think that God is not hearing. Hallelujah. God has no respect of persons. The same God that hears me said he'll hear you! Did you clean up? Glory be to God.

Your problem is that you want to stay with Satan and be a hindrance. But the devil is a liar. Glory be to God!

And I execute judgment! I execute God's judgment on everyone that want to hinder me, that want to hinder God's people in this place! God give you no rest! Amen. Not a day. Give you no rest, until you humble yourself. And if you won't humble, then God cast your soul where it belongs! In the wrath of God!

Amen. I declare war! Praise God in the highest! Hallelujah. Glory to God in the highest. Hallelujah. I know my God hears me. Thank you, Jesus! Thank you, Jesus! Thank you, Jesus!

There is nothing or nobody that I love more than my God. And no one is standing in the way of what God has ordained. Praise God in the highest. The devil is a liar.

Amen. And the truth is not in him. You hear me today! Praise God. Praise God. I make no, no excuse for anyone, and I apologize to no man. This God I serve, said, preach his word! Glory be to God. And Execute His Word written!

I'm not here just to preach. I'm here to execute God's judgment upon the ungodly and the disobedient who have played church for years. In and out, in and out, fooling around, fooling around, want to commit adultery, want to commit fornication, want to do witchcraft, and all this garbage. And then come as if you've done nothing and sit with the saints… God forbid! God forbid! Praise God in the highest. Praise our God! Praise our God!

And don't you think I'm that stupid, praise God, to think that even your offspring is going to win me over. They're your offspring, Amen, just like you! Clean up! Glory be to God.

You know God spoke to my heart. He said,

> "I have greater things than even your grandchildren. Come after me."

You see what I'm saying. For years, I longed to be a grandmother, and God blessed me. I've got three grandchildren. Amen.

And I'm just glorying in them all these precious little ones. And God said,

> "I have greater things for you than these grandchildren."

Knowing how much I love them, and He loves them greater than I could ever. But he has greater things…Glory to God. And I must ready myself after those greater things. So don't you think that even your little ones are going to be a hindrance in my life? Amen. It won't be. It won't be.

Glory to God. Glory to God. Glory to my God. I love him. Amen. Thank you, Jesus. Thank you, Jesus. I'm only a fanatic for Jesus. Everybody's a fanatic of something. Amen. But I'm a fan of Jesus. Praise God. I live for him. Glory to his name. I want my offspring saved. I want them full of God. I want them to love God. So I must be about my Father's business that they may have the blessings of God and the anointing of God upon their lives as well as mine. Amen. Glory to Jesus.

I want you to know. I want that to be crystal clear in your mind, that I love God only. Above anything else. Thank you, Jesus. Please understand that. I will not apologize. Glory to Jesus.

One was in our home, acting up. And being foolish. And being used by the devil, and trying to overthrow the family. And they had a little one. She was there in the home, and she went and had the baby. And brought the baby back home. And we went wild over that baby, oh, we love children, we love children. Praise God.

And in her wickedness, the mother in her wickedness thought that because we love that baby, we'd be blind to her. You know I sought the Lord. And I sought the Lord.

And I warned that mother. And I warned that mother. And she kept on in her wickedness, and kept being used of Satan against my family. And I said, Lord, alright, you just give me to know what to do. The Lord said,

"Tell her to take her baby. And get out of here."

And told me where the apartment was. And told her to get there, go today, I told her. And she said the apartment, the apartment might be registered to somebody. I said uh uh. The Lord said it's open. You get that baby, and get out of here. Glory to God in the highest. God is God. And today she's in our midst, saved! Saved! Cause she knew I wasn't playing. Glory to God in the highest. But she got her baby that day. And got out of there.

So don't you start using that. Uh, uh. Ain't nothing gonna separate me from the God I love. Praise God in the heights. Nothing! Nothing! I start weighing out who my God is. And what he is to me. And I start weighing out who man is. Uh uh. I'll take my God! I'll take my God! Glory be to God.

And believe me. This is not coming out of faint lips, honey. I've been tried in the fire. Glory be to God. There was a time when everything left me. And I'm on my knees all by myself. So I know. I know where my bread is buttered. Glory to God in the highest. Thank you, Jesus.

And you gotta get likewise. For God I live. For God I die. Amen. For the blessings. Amen. Thank you for the answers to prayer. Amen. But for God I live…For God I live… And for God I die. Blessed be the name of the Lord.

Thank you, Jesus. We gotta know where we stand. God's gonna test every one of us. All those years I was saved, and when I had to leave my 10 children and go to Africa. After we had done the will of God, after… I can only answer for myself. After I had done the will of God. We were leaving that first airport up in the plane. Going up, and the Lord said.

"Now I know that thou lovest me."

What? Now, you know? But I knew what he meant. I knew what he meant. That I left all, I left my little heartthrobs. All 10 of them. Amen. And left them with no money. You understand? Only a crazy person would do that. Amen. A fool. And I was a fool for Christ.

But I did it. And God never let them go lacking. God fed them every day. Fed them every day. Praise God in the highest. And at that time, I had no money to pay any mortgage. We stayed in that house 18 months without paying any mortgage. Amen. I just stretched out on Jesus. And no matter what anyone else said, no matter how the devil would, would try to buffet my mind. God said,

"The house is yours. The house is yours. Go!"

Glory to God, and that I did. I did because Jesus said, Go. Amen. And today the house is still there, and we're still in it. Praise God in the highest! The children are all grown. My baby's 17 years old. Glory to God. God's faithful! And he's true!

Praise God in the highest. Praise you, Jesus. Praise you, Jesus. Amen, Amen. Bless His holy name.

I've seen the marvelous hand of God, down through the years; He can fail. God can't fail us when we dare take Him at his word. Amen. He is the Word of God. And what he says, you believe him. And don't try to figure out how He's going to do it, you just get up and do what he says.

Praise God in the highest. Bless our king. Bless our king. Our savior divine. Oh, what a mighty God. Holy Jesus!

All right. In verse 4 of Revelation chapter 20.

> *And I saw thrones, and they sat upon them, and judgment was given unto them: and I saw the souls of them that were beheaded for the witness of Jesus, and for the word of God, and which had not worshipped the beast, neither his image, neither had received his mark upon their foreheads, or in their hands; and they lived and reigned with Christ a thousand years.*

These are the ones that were left to go through the tribulation. But they refused to receive the mark of the beast. Amen. They didn't make it to the marriage supper. But they didn't give up and betray Jesus for a morsel of bread.

Don't you know that those who will not receive the mark of the beast will be those that cannot buy anything unless they have the number 666? Amen. Saints, it's going to be a terrible time for those who refuse to be discipled now.

Some will come to an awakening during that great trial of tribulation. While we are home at the marriage supper. Amen.

But some will receive the mark of the beast and will never have a chance to be saved, ever again. They'll be doomed while they're yet breathing on this earth. It's going to be a horrible time. A horrible time for those who would not receive the mark of the beast, and a horrible time for those who do.

The difference is… Those who refuse to receive the mark of the beast have assuredly eternal life. They would have to have gone through the tribulation to be made pure. Amen. And they shall reign with Christ for a thousand years, but they will be even yet in a mortal body. And some in a glorified body. We who have gone to the marriage supper shall come back with Jesus, with those great armies, in a glorified body.

But those who would not allow the trumpet of God to awaken them shall be awakened through the tribulation. And shall go through great persecution. Now the choice is yours. Are you going to be foolish enough to take that chance? Will you be that crazy? Your answer should be no emphatically!

Glory to God. I'm going home at the first call. Glory be to God. So our ears must be circumcised. Praise the Lord. Don't you know that we're going out of here, and there's going to be a lot of lies said about us, you know. What really happened in our disappearance… But we'll be home.

Glory to God in the highest. But when Jesus comes back, the whole world will know it. Because out of heaven, Jesus will be the main leader. His vesture dipped in blood, on a white horse. And his tongue like a sword spewing out judgments against his enemies. And he's going to tread the wine press in his wrath. Glory be to God. And the armies of Heaven shall follow him. And I've said ever since I was a new convert. "Lord, I want to be on my horse." Amen. And I really believe that's why God has allowed many wars to come against me. Because he wants to train me, Amen, for that day when I ride out of heaven following Jesus. Amen.

I'm going to fight like I never fought. Praise God in the highest. Every enemy I've had to say, God, bless you… I'm going to bring him down. Glory be to God. Everyone who refused to be saved. I'm going to bring 'em down with a sword of God. Amen. That my God shall entrust me with. Praise God in the highest.

Amen. Vengeance. Belongeth. Unto God. Hallelujah. We got to walk lowly and meekly now towards man. Never will I be humble or meek towards any devil. Glory be to God in the highest. I must grin, I must bear it, and I'm saying "God bless you, enemy." Now, not later.

You don't humble yourself to my God. Amen. If you don't love me, as my God loves me. I'm going to have your head. Glory be to God. I'm going to trample you under my feet. I'm going to see that you're ashes under my feet. Praise God. I know how to wait…

There's a lot of things that, when I moved into our home, amen, that needed to be done. And some of those things are yet to be done. And I'm telling you, I know how to be patient. I know how to wait.

So, I know how to wait until my change comes, praise God. You're going to bow at my Lord's feet. You're going to bow.

Praise God. You can traffic with the devil if you please. Amen. But I'm going to have his head, and I'm going to have yours. Glory to God in the highest. That's the way it stands. And when I leave this pulpit. I'll grab you, I'll hug you, I'll kiss you, I'll laugh with you.

But you better believe what I say here, I mean. Glory to God. And it won't change unless you change. Hallelujah. Because I know where my help comes from. I know where my help is, it's in the Lord. It's in the Lord. Alright. In verse 5, he says,

> *But the rest of the dead lived not again until the thousand years were finished.*

See, because they had died and they were staying dead, until God had done the work of a thousand years.

> *This is the first resurrection. Blessed and holy is he that hath part in the first resurrection:*

You hear me? That's us, that's going into the marriage supper. And believe me, God has his people everywhere that's going to be ready. Glory be to God. God will not be defeated. Amen. Nor in rank or in number.

> *on such the second death hath no power, but they shall be priests of God and of Christ, and shall reign with him a thousand years. And when the thousand years are expired, Satan shall be loosed out of his prison, and shall go out to deceive*

See, he doesn't know how to stop, he's driven with a spirit of madness. And I'm finding that his servants are the same way as human servants. They don't know when to stop.

They have no sense whatsoever. Glory be to God. They just don't know when to stop. And I mark them, I mark it down on my invisible calendar. And I'm remembering, I'm remembering. You won't stop, you won't stop. And I'll keep smiling at you. Until I go to war, glory be to God.

> *and shall go out to deceive the nations which are in the four quarters of the earth, Gog and Magog, to gather them together to battle: the number of whom is as the sand of the sea. And they went up on the breadth of the earth, and compassed the camp of the saints about, and the beloved city: and fire came down from God out of heaven,*

See satan went to declare war on the saints, went to declare war on Jerusalem, the holy city. Went to declare war on that which belongs to God. Amen. And fire, the wrath of God. You see?

> *and fire came down from God out of heaven,*

Not the beast now, from God Almighty.

> *and devoured them. And the devil that deceived them was cast into the lake of fire and brimstone, where the beast and the false prophet are, and shall be tormented day and night for ever and ever.*

See, the beast was the one that ruled during the seven-year persecution, and the false prophet. You see? And they've already been cast into the pit. And now Satan is being loosed so he can get his final damnation. You understand this? His final reward is hellfire, the pit and brimstone. Amen.

And you might say, well, he sure had a good time making war on the saints. Uh uh. He's miserable; he's never at peace. Don't you ever believe his lies; he's never at peace.

He's tormented day and night. You don't believe it? Cast the devil out. Cast him out of somebody, you'll find out how tormented he is. Amen. Verse 10,

> *And the devil that deceived them was cast into the lake of fire and brimstone, where the beast and the false prophet are, and shall be tormented day and night for ever and ever.*

> *And I saw a great white throne, and him that sat on it, from whose face the earth and the heaven fled away;*

The earth and the heaven fled away.

> *and there was found no place for them. And I saw the dead, small and great, stand before God; and the books were opened:*

This is not the book of life now.

The books were opened. Which is the book of life. And the dead were judged.

There is not only the book of life. But all the things that were said are recorded. There's a certain book of things that were said. Amen. Of the saints, every word, every praise, every thanksgiving. Amen. All the things that we talked about concerning God… According to the book, according

to Malachi, there's a book, a certain book that's been
printed on our behalf, right now. Amen.

God hears it, and it's being recorded. Praise God. Every
good thing. That's why we've got to order our conversation
aright. We've got to do it, saints. Amen. Stay full of praise.
There's a spirit of madness out here, and we have to stay
full of praise. Thinking on the mighty things of God. And
speak those things.

Encouraging one another. Amen. The saints, the true saints.
Encouraging them, amen, and exhorting them and one
another. Then all of this is written on our behalf. Then we
see the book of life. And it says,

> *and another book was opened, which is the book of
> life: and the dead were judged out of those things
> which were written in the books, according to their
> works.*

Let me turn you to Malachi that you might see what I'm
really saying here. I feel led of the Lord to take you there.
That's the last book in the Old Testament, praise God in the
highest. Malachi, the third chapter, verse 16.

> *Then they that feared the LORD spake often one to
> another: and the LORD hearkened, and heard it,
> and a book of remembrance was written before him
> for them that feared the LORD, and that thought
> upon his name. And they shall be mine, saith
> the LORD of hosts, in that day when I make up my
> jewels; and I will spare them, as a man spareth his
> own son that serveth him.*

And down in chapter 4, verse 1.

> *For, behold, the day cometh, that shall burn as an oven; and all the proud, yea, and all that do wickedly, shall be stubble: and the day that cometh shall burn them up, saith the LORD of hosts, that it shall leave them neither root nor branch. But unto you that fear my name shall the Sun*

Capital S. un,

> *of righteousness arise with healing in his wings.*

So you see how the angel stood in the sun.

> *and ye shall go forth, and grow up as calves of the stall.*

We have great and mighty promises that await us; let's not fall short of those promises. Let's enter in, let's receive everything that God has in store for us now, and in the future. It's ours if we dare be obedient to who He is, and what he says.

We must put him on. The word of God commends us, saying, quit ye like men, put on the Lord Jesus Christ.

Finally, my brethren, whatsoever things are pure, just, true, Amen, virtuous. Everything that is written in that eighth verse that's putting on The Lord Jesus Christ. And we shall be owned by him in that day.

And we shall be preserved, only if we have put him on in our character. If we put Jesus character in our being. And choose everything he says. Do everything He requires. And he's not going to put any grievous thing on us.

Whatever he commands, we can do it. By the power of God that works in us. His power works continually in us, enabling us to obey him. And when he comes He's coming looking for his fruit. Not the gifts, not the gifts, but the fruit of righteousness. Hallelujah.

All right, I'll finish this, and we'll close. Verse eight, I read this before, but I want you to see,

> *and shall go out to deceive the nations which are in the four quarters of the earth, Gog and Magog, to gather them together to battle: the number of whom is as the sand of the sea. And they went up on the breadth of the earth, and compassed the camp of the saints about, and the beloved city: and fire came down from God out of heaven, and devoured them. And the devil that deceived them was cast into the lake of fire and brimstone, where the beast and the false prophet are, and shall be tormented day and night for ever and ever.*
>
> *And I saw a great white throne, and him that sat on it, from whose face the earth and the heaven fled away; and there was found no place for them. And I saw the dead, small and great, stand before God; and the books were opened: and another book was opened, which is the book of life:*

Another book, which is the book of life. But there was a greater volume of books, Amen.

and the dead were judged out of those things which were written in the books, according to their works. And the sea gave up the dead which were in it; and death and hell delivered up the dead which were in them:

Everything has got to obey God, even death and hell!

and they were judged every man according to their works.

In other words, they're not going to be hid by hell nor death. Death and hell and the sea got to surrender the dead that's in it to God to be judged. It's a terrible time coming for those who are disobedient. God help us!

And death and hell were cast into the lake of fire. This is the second death. And whosoever was not found written in the book of life was cast into the lake of fire.

Amen, won't be water like in Noah's day, but fire and brimstone. But we who love God and follow Him relentlessly, faithfully, we shall be ever with the Lord.

Let us stand.

Glory to God. We thank you, thank you for your word. Thank you for putting fear and trembling in our hearts. Thank you that we are not fools and blind, but we know and understand who you are.

And that your word is true, and every word that proceeds out of your mouth. You shall surely bring to pass. You will not disannul it, you will not alter it. And God forbid that we even try. Lord, we know you're coming, and we want to be found ready. We are preparing to meet you, as the book of Revelation says, his wife has made herself ready.

We know that there's no gender in you. There's neither male nor female. We're spirit beings, souls you're looking at. Praise God in the highest. And we are making ourselves ready to ever be with you and to sit down at your banqueting table.

Living In His Beauty

First Aired August 2nd, 1998

We give God the praise and the honor for being who He is and for blessing us to be His, to belong to him. We're thanking God for all the prayers that you've prayed for us, and we're coveting your prayers continually. God is so good. Every mouth that knows Christ as their savior has to agree and has to say, has to confess, God is so good and merciful. Bless his holy name.

Let us pray. Father, we thank you for your goodness, and boldly we come into your presence in the precious and mighty name of Jesus Christ. Thanking you for this day that you have made. Thanking you for another opportunity, Father, amen, to speak your word. Lord, knowing that we know nothing of ourselves, we are trusting that your blessed Holy Spirit will give utterance this day.

Enlighten our eyes that we might see and our ears unstop that we might hear and melt our hearts before you to this day, that thy will, thy precious and holy will, will be done and made known and working your mighty work through us and in us. Have thine own way, thy kingdom come, thy will be done on earth as it is in heaven. You taught us to pray.

Let your precious anointing flow from bosom to bosom and from breast to breast in each heart and each mind. Watch upon your word and perform it in us, we pray. Beat back the forces of hell that would come to steal your word out of our hearts.

Bind the hand of the wicked one. Bring down his strongholds. Bring down his walls, Father. Bring them down in thine authority and in thy most powerful name. And bless the work of thy hands. Bless us in Zion this day. We ask it all in the precious name of Jesus Christ and let your word fall on good ground. Amen and amen.

The fifth chapter of Saint Matthew, the Beatitudes of Christ Jesus.

I'll back up into the fourth chapter first. In the fourth chapter, we find that Jesus Christ was driven into the wilderness by the Spirit of God, the Holy Spirit, to be tempted by the devil. In other words, to prove to the enemy that he could withstand him no matter what. And Jesus withstood him, praise God.

And after this, after he had overcome every temptation and beat back the forces of hell in Satan, the word of God says in the 13th verse,

> *and leaving Nazareth, he came and dwelt in Capernaum, which is upon the sea coast, in the borders of Zabulon and Nephthalim: that it might be fulfilled which was spoken by Esaias the prophet, saying, The land of Zabulon, and the land of Nephthalim, By the way of the sea, beyond Jordan, Galilee of the Gentiles; The people which sat in darkness Saw great light;*

Jesus is that light, Amen.

> *And to them which sat in the region and shadow of death Light is sprung up. From that time Jesus began to preach, and to say, Repent: for the kingdom of heaven is at hand.*

So we see by the writings of Matthew that Jesus declares, and those who knew him declared that Jesus is that light shining in darkness. Praise God.

And even the people that sat in regions of death itself, the Lord, being that great light, shone unto them. And he is yet shining to those that are sitting in darkness that they might come unto him and walk in the light, which is the way to heaven. Glory to his name.

When he tells us, Jesus said then, and he is saying today, repent for the kingdom of heaven is at hand. And in the fifth chapter,

> *And seeing the multitudes, he went up into a mountain: and when he was set, his disciples came unto him: and he opened his mouth,*

He opened his mouth…

> *and taught them, saying,*

> *Blessed are the poor in spirit: for their's is the kingdom of heaven.*

When you realize that you are poor and you need help, then you call on his name. You go unto God. And the Lord said theirs, for theirs is the kingdom of heaven. The Lord will not withhold any good thing from those who walk upright before him.

> *Blessed are they that mourn: for they shall be comforted.*

Whatever you might be going through, whatever it is, and surely God's people are going through these are the last days, and they are most evil. And many, many will have to mourn, grieved in spirit.

But the Lord says they shall be comforted. Jesus says they shall be comforted. Isn't it marvelous to know that God cares so much that he comforts you. He's that concerned.

And not only will he comfort, not only will his loving arms be wrapped around and about you and speaking comfortable words to you, words of encouragement, He is with you always.

> *Blessed are the meek: for they shall inherit the earth.*

Blessed are the meek, for they shall inherit the earth. One day there shall be a new heaven and a new earth. And this is why the Lord is telling us to hold on.

See, this is the attitude that God wants us to live in daily. Holding on no matter how vehemently, trials will come against us to beat us down. We're trusting in the Lord to keep us day by day and in our daily activity with one another.

And especially with those that are yet in the world. God says blessed are the meek, for they shall inherit the earth.

Many times, even on your jobs, others who are not worthy will prosper ahead of you. They will gain that position that you are qualified for. Glory to God, and in other walks of life.

Amen. What you should have is things like the wicked is gaining day by day, but it's okay. It's all right, this world is not our home. The meek shall inherit the earth. If you just stay in the right attitude, stay in a right spirit, in a right spirit. Praise God. That's meekness. Because meekness will teach you patience, how to wait on the Lord.

Blessed are the meek, for they shall inherit the earth. Everybody today is wanting things right now, right now. I deserve it, give it to me. If you don't give it, I'll take it. But that's the wrong attitude. That's an evil spirit. That's an evil heart. The Lord said, blessed are the meek. Those that are in a right spirit, for they shall inherit the earth. You can rest assured, you will inherit the earth right along with the others that have walked upright before God and have made the Lord their trust.

> *Blessed are they which do hunger and thirst after righteousness: for they shall be filled.*

And this is something that we must dwell on daily. Precious ones, God wants us to hunger and thirst after the things of God. Amen. After the spiritual blessings of the Lord. But too long, too long, God's people have been taught how to gain and how to believe for the things of this world.

Things of this world are coming to an end. Glory be to God. And I would go even further to say it's going up in smoke. Praise God.

But they that endure to the end, the same shall be saved, the Bible tells us. So we are to hunger and thirst after the righteousness of God. Go after that which is pleasing in the eyes of God. So that means we have to stay in communion daily with God. We have to talk, we have to converse, we have to communicate with God, our maker, our Father. And Jesus Christ, our Lord and way maker. Praise His holy name.

Jesus is that way. He's that light to show us the way to the Father's heart and to the Father's throne. Praises unto God.

Isn't it marvelous that Jesus Christ is that door, and He has given us access to the Father and the throne of God by him, by Jesus Christ, that open door. He's an open door, He will not close the door on you if you come in faith, believing.

He will not cast you away from him. Glory to his name. He is eager for you to come and lay hold upon the promises of God, which are yea and amen to them that believe God.

Blessed are they which do hunger and thirst after righteousness. And he didn't stop there. He said they, for they shall be filled, for they shall be filled. If you're hungering after the righteousness of God and thirsting, amen, God will fill you through and through with his righteousness. Glory to his name with his whole being.

> *Blessed are the merciful: for they shall obtain mercy.*

The right attitude towards one another, glory, Hallelujah. Not me first, and what's left you can have. Amen. But showing mercy, even as God has shown us mercy and he does daily, doesn't he? He shows us mercy, and great is his mercy towards us. And with that same mercy that we are recipients of, God wants us to manifest to others, our fellow men.

Praise God, whether they are right or wrong, show mercy, show mercy. Because whatever we meet out, it's going to be meted back to us again. Blessed are the merciful, for they shall obtain mercy.

Now the devil would tell you to strike back, get even. Don't, don't let them get away with it and so forth. But the Lord said, blessed are the merciful, for they shall obtain mercy. And show me one person who has never needed mercy shown to them. We all need mercy in one sense or another. As long as we live, we need the mercies of God and his favor upon us.

He says,

> *Blessed are the pure in heart: for they shall see God.*

Amen, there's mercy, and there's hungering after righteousness, but those that will see God are the ones whose heart is pure. No guile, Hallelujah, God wants us to have a what? A pure heart in the eyes of God.

Praise the Lord of hosts. Our hearts have to be right. And not only right, but pure. No spot, no blemish. What a mighty God, for they shall see God. They, the one with that pure heart, whom God calls pure. For they shall see God. That's a promise.

Look forward to it. Amen. Blessed are the peacemakers, for they shall be called the children of God. And this is so greatly needed today. Even amongst the children of God, we need to know that God is a God of peace. Amen.

In our everyday living, God wants us to live with peace. Praise the Lord, whatever it takes to obtain peace in a righteous manner, get peace. Peace! Amen, peace between one another, peace in your heart with God. Peace in your everyday living with one another. Peace when you see others at odds against one another.

You strive for peace! Don't keep the confusion. Don't keep the contention. Don't keep the strife going. You seek the peace of God. You might be despised because you want peace. But you want peace because you want to be that peacemaker in the eyes of God. God is a God of peace.

Bless his holy name. And whatever you have to do to wrought peace, make sure you get it. Seek peace, pursue peace. Go after peace. Amen. You go before the peacemaker. The peacemaker is God. He's the one who's going to bring peace in strife and confusion. The Lord will bring peace.

He'll right the wrong. He'll set in order that which is out of order. This is the way of the Most High God. Hallelujah. And saints of God, if we don't have that attitude, we'll have a wrong spirit. Amen. Seek the peace of God. It's not just, 'well, I'm right, and they're wrong.' Or 'perhaps I was wrong.' No, you seek peace; God wants peace!

How many times has the Lord led me even to my bosom enemies to tell them, I love you. Glory be to God. The self, the old self (is saying) 'No, no, no. I don't think I should do it.' But God says, 'Do it, do it.' And you already know what their attitude is going to be. They'll get self-righteous on you. They'll fold their arms, and when you see them again, they pretend like they never saw you. Glory be to God. But you go for peace. Amen. Don't do them any harm. Go for peace.

The Bible says, if it be possible, as much as lieth within you, live peaceably with all men, Praise God. See them as God sees them, I don't care what they've done. See man as God sees them. They have a soul, praise the Lord of hosts.

> *Blessed are the peacemakers: for they shall be called the children of God.*

Don't you want to really be a child of God? Children of God? The answer is yes and amen. Anybody in their right mind want to be called a child of God. Well, this is how you're known to be a child of God. This is what Jesus, not only the master teacher, but the Lord of Hosts, has spoken. Hallelujah!

> *Blessed are they which are persecuted for righteousness' sake:*

You even talk about peace and you're counted as a busybody. Amen. But Jesus said, if you're persecuted for righteousness' sake, blessed are ye.

> *for their's is the kingdom of heaven.*

You have access to God at all times. And isn't it marvelous to live where you know you have access to the throne of grace? The word of God says, come boldly to the throne of grace, that you might obtain mercy and find grace to help in the time of need. To help? We need God's help, don't we? Praise God.

No matter how long that we know we have walked with the Lord or how the time that we have known the Lord, the days or the years or the months or whatever, no matter how short or how long we have known the Lord, we want to know that we are walking before him unto all pleasing.

And we can please God. We can please the heart of God. Just obey his word. Accept his loving gift, Jesus Christ, and walk in Him. Go after the kingdom of heaven, not just impart, but the whole, continually going after the kingdom of heaven. Those things that God has placed in his kingdom… It's yours. Amen. Hallelujah.

If you are persecuted for righteousness sake, theirs is the kingdom of heaven.

> *Blessed are ye, when men shall revile you, and persecute you, and shall say all manner of evil against you falsely, for my sake.*

All because you carry the name of Jesus Christ, and you are standing upright with Christ. You have harmony with Christ for his sake. You're bearing these things that man, this persecution that man will bring against you, and they'll revile you with their tongues. They'll cast out your name as evil. The Lord said, you're blessed. Blessed are you. Marvelous, isn't it? Glory be to God.

Wake up, Zion, and hear the word of the Lord. Blessed are ye when men shall revile you and persecute you. They won't just stop speaking ugly things against you. Amen. Because you love Jesus and God's mercies are abundantly upon you, his favor. Amen. Because you love.

But you have the kingdom of God at hand. The kingdom of heaven is yours. You're a child of God. Amen. And more than that, more than that, the Lord tells us to rejoice, rejoice.

When I would read this, and I didn't know how to go through trials and didn't know how to bear persecutions in the manner that the Lord wanted me to, in the right attitude. I would read this, and I would say, 'Oh, Lord God, I'm not there, I'm just not there, I don't have it.' God loves an honest heart.

But the Lord was teaching me. He was breaking down the self-will in me. Amen. And destroying that which was displeasing to God by allowing persecutions to come. Hallelujah. And in doing so, he was establishing me in the righteousness of God.

He would let me see the error of my ways, not at what somebody else was doing to me, but me. He was letting me see self as the greatest enemy of all. Because self cannot please God. And Jesus said, deny self. Deny self, pick up your cross, and follow me. Your obligation is to follow me.

Leave that one that's persecuting you in the hands of God. Go on, go on to perfection. Go after Jesus Christ, the most perfect one. And no matter where we go to in the Bible, we cannot see any fault with Jesus Christ. He handled himself perfectly, being full of the Holy Ghost and led by the Holy Ghost as he walked this earth.

So we have a perfect example before us. Blessed are we, he says, when men shall revile you and persecute you and shall say all manner of evil against you falsely for my sake.

I am going through precious ones. I'm going through things that in times past I'd said I would actually kill before I'd go through it. But God killed self, amen. I have gone across town with weapons to destroy a person's life when I was in the Southland because somebody had something evil to say about me. Oh, but God taught me your way is not my way.

And how many times have I had to go to my knees for strength to endure when persecution would come against me? I never thought that I could laugh at any lie that was ever told to me. But precious ones, as we endure and God's grace is multiplied unto us, we can laugh at the devil. We can go through, and we don't have to go through with a broken-down heart.

The Lord will fix our hearts, and he will regulate our minds, and he will make us steadfast and unmovable before God and man. Hallelujah. And certainly in the face of the devil, God would give us strength and power, his overcoming power to endure those revilings that come against us, those lies that are spoken against us.

We must have the right attitude. Praise his holy name. God is for us as long as we are obedient to his word. And we find ourselves short. How many times have I found myself short of the word of God? Amen. But just be honest, God blesses those who are honest, and the seed of God is sown in honest hearts.

When we find ourselves, oh God, it's not in me, but create thy word in me... IN me! Help me to be a doer, Lord, I cannot, outside of you, do this. I cannot obey your word, but you in me, I can and I shall. It shall be done.

See, that's trusting God, that's seeing your weakness and your lack, but also seeing God's faithfulness and his strength. God will see us through. The Lord says, rejoice and be exceeding glad. I've seen the times when I say, I can't rejoice over that. No way can I rejoice. Lord, you saw what they did to me. Lord God, you heard that lie. Lord, they shouldn't be able to get away with that, Lord.

No one's getting away with anything. God is molding his own. God is shaping the hearts of his own. God is creating in us a right spirit. God sees that the day of the wicked is coming, and it's not long. Praise God. But honey, go ahead and receive that that God has for you. You need his blessings. You need God's blessings every day.

When you say I'm blessed, I'm blessed. Be sure it's not just God's mercies upon you. Be blessed to be established in the righteousness of God with an attitude that only God can approve. The world will not approve this kind of attitude. The world tells you eye for eye, amen, tooth for tooth.

 And they're trying to mesmerize your mind to overcome you to get what you have. But you still have to have the right attitude. You still have to live in a state of forgiveness. Praise the Lord most, amen. You have to forgive those. I mean, they'll take your home. They'll take your belongings.

They'll take that which you inherited. Glory to God. They'll take that which is intended for you. Jesus said, if they take your coat, give them your cloak also. Give it to them. The Lord has plenty.

The earth is the Lord's and the fullness thereof. It's the Lord's, amen. In a house, whatever it's made out of, God's got plenty of timber yet in the forest. He's got all the gold and all the silver. Not only in Fort Knox, he's got it all around. He's got gold that has not even yet been discovered in the earth.

So why are you going to cry over that that has been taken from you? Amen. As long as you've got God, you've got everything. For theirs is the kingdom of heaven! Bless his holy name. Everything that God has is yours. We are heirs and joint heirs with Jesus Christ.

And just keep on waiting and keep on looking up. Praise God. Jesus is coming for his own, and you'll see what you have. Praise God. This earth is going to pass away with a great heat. It's going to pass away!

But they that know the Lord, we shall stand forever. Hold on. Help is on the way!

Amen and Amen!

Time to Pray

First aired Dec 10th, 2000

Praise God in the highest. We thank the Lord for this opportunity once more and again to come to you by the way of radio, and we thank God for God himself because he is the great I am. We thank him for his mercies abundantly that he has shown unto us the children of men.

We see the glory of God in the midst of chaos, and that's what I want to talk about today. God's glory in the midst of chaos. In Jeremiah, the ninth chapter, you who have your Bibles, please turn with me.

Let us pray. Precious Father, we thank you for this opportunity that you've given us once more and again to make your voice known, to bring forth your word and bring it forth unhindered. Bring it forth on the power and the unction of the Holy Ghost and bind up every opposition that would fight against your word.

Bring down the spirits of rebellion that would deny your truth and deny your presence in the name of Jesus Christ, thy son, and pour out your spirit of understanding and knowledge, and power. Amen. In the lives of your people.

Praise God. Help us, Lord, to receive by truth. Amen. In Jesus glorious name, bring deliverance to the captives and those that sit in darkness. Let them see your great light. Thy truth is light, and thy truth is life everlasting. Hallelujah. Jesus Christ is the truth. He is that way. He is life indeed.

Help us to hear your truth and abide therein and reprove us, Lord. Reprove us wherever we need reproof and build us up on thy most holy faith that we may walk upright before you and to keep your statutes and your judgments to abide in your truth in the glorious and most powerful name, Jesus Christ, amen and amen.

The ninth chapter of Jeremiah reads,

> *Oh that my head were waters, and mine eyes a fountain of tears, that I might weep day and night for the slain of the daughter of my people! Oh that I had in the wilderness a lodging place of wayfaring men; that I might leave my people, and go from them! for they be all adulterers, an assembly of treacherous men. And they bend their tongues like their bow for lies: but they are not valiant for the truth upon the earth;*

Remember that phrase, but they are not valiant for the truth upon the earth,

> *or they proceed from evil to evil, and they know not me, saith the LORD.*

God, knowing the heart of man, I've heard people say this over and over. God knows my heart. Yes, he does. And God has a way of revealing the heart of man. Jesus tells us in the New Testament that ugly and wicked things proceed from the heart, the mouth speaks what's in the heart.

If evil things come from the mouth, it's because the heart is evil. If the heart is full of light and truth and love, then

good things are coming forth from the mouth of that
person.

The Lord tells us in the Word that the people are not valiant
for the truth. The truth is most important in the eyes of
God. He's a God of truth. God… this is one thing he cannot
do, God can not lie. There's no lie in him. He is not a liar.
There is no lie in God's spirit. He cannot speak it because
it's not in his spirit. He's all truth; everything he says is true.
Praise his holy name. Hallelujah.

The Lord says,

> *for they be all adulterers, an assembly of*
> *treacherous men. And they bend their*
> *tongues like their bow for lies:*

But they say, because of the treachery in the heart,
treachery in the heart, not valiant to speak truth, don't want
to know the truth. Because if we speak truth, that brings
responsibility for uprightness. And man doesn't want the
uprightness of God.

Many do not want to live holy and righteous and true.
These are all requirements of a born-again individual. God
requires it. In the old nature, it's impossible. No matter how
gracious or full of goodness a person can be, if they are not
born again, they're going to miss whatever God is after.

We must be born again to take on the nature, to take on the
conduct of our Lord and Savior, Jesus Christ. We cannot be
righteous, void of God. And this is what God is saying. And
he saw this back in the time that Jeremiah was a prophet,
and Jeremiah had to cry out against the wickedness and the

ugliness that he saw in man because God had spoken these things, and Jeremiah had to speak.

And man has not changed. I don't care what hour, what day, what generation, what year, what nationality, what country. Man is the same all over. So God's word is on record for every man to take heed. This is why the word of God was written. It's for our edification, it's for our reproof, it's for our rebuke, it's to teach us the way of the Lord.

And it's also written here, the failure of men, that we might know what God is against. There are examples to us that we are not to follow their failure; we are to follow Jesus Christ, who has never failed, cannot fail. Praise God in the highest. But I want to concentrate on truth. God says man is not valiant for the truth, for the truth.

They bend the bow of their mouth, their tongue to speak lies. And see with lies comes corruption and guile. It comes evil because lies are never good, no matter what intention you may have. A little white lie, a little white lie is a lie. And that little lie may grow to be vastly large, you see. So you don't start with any little sin. It's going to grow and multiply to greater sin.

We cannot order our lives without Christ, without God in us, enabling us, empowering us. And even with Christ in us, we still must hear the Holy Spirit; we must be guided by the Holy Spirit to lead us and guide us into the truth of the Almighty.

And to love the truth, the Bible says love the truth and sell it not. Don't just sell out for yourself. Don't sell out for anyone else. God is looking on us. He's looking on our nation. He's seeing what has brought this nation to the chaos that we are in today.

Man thought that on November the 7th, everybody would know exactly who would be the president, the next president-elect of America, but it didn't happen, hasn't happened yet, because this is God's timing to show America her ills, her treachery, her lies, her deceit, her debates.

They say arguments, God says debates. Her murderous ways, her conniving ways, her skill to do wickedness. We see lawyers, I say many times, they're paid lying mouthpieces, standing before the judge and twisting the truth, saying evil things, trying to persuade men to believe a lie.

God is tired of it. And believe it or not, precious ones, we're standing in the judgment of God already. God is weighing our sins as a nation before all the world. God showed me right after the so-called election of the next president. God showed me a scale and the balances of the scale, and we as a nation were found wanting before God, because the leaders, the leaders of our nation, are corrupt.

Not just from the high office, it's all the way down. Man has forgotten God, and man wants to continue to murder babies. They want to continue to do ugly things with the same sex. And God is saying, I've had enough, because all of this wickedness has been shown into all the world.

Many nations are looking to our nation as an example. And we've shown other nations just how corrupt this nation really is.

And now all these things that we're learning that go on behind the scenes in the courtrooms and in the judges' chambers, and you name it, we're seeing it coming out in the open. What's done in darkness shall come to light. The things that are behind the scenes before everyone's eyes.

Because God is at work, and one thinks today they've got the presidency. The next one thinks tomorrow they've got the presidency. God is weighing us. God is looking on his people to change our ways, to start looking to man to get what we want.

God is our source, and God is our supply. And no matter who is in office, we have still got to look unto the Lord, our God, by whom we are named. Praise the Lord of hosts. Man is man, hallelujah. But God is God, and he is not like man. God is righteous altogether.

Man may be righteous in their thought partly, but God is altogether righteous, and no one can deceive him. No one has the power to lie to God and deceive him or to lie to humanity and deceive humanity. No one can do this. Amen.

Without God on our side, we would have been swallowed up long ago. We have many ills and many enemies in this nation that will rob us of our privacy, that would rob us of our help and our strength, our mental health, our physical strength, our spiritual health, and our spiritual strength.

There are many wars against us in this nation, not only in this world, but in this nation. And I, as a minister of the gospel of Jesus Christ and a prophetess in the room of God, I must tell you his truth. No matter what it costs me, I may have to pay with my life. Well, it's all right. But God's truth must be, it must go forth, and somebody must heed the word of God. God loves the truth. God loves me because he knows I'm going to speak his truth. He can trust me because I am going to say it exactly like God gives it to me.

It's not Republican, it's not Democrat, it's God that we should look to! And God help us for leaning on the arms of the flesh.

I see madness in it all. Now, I know God is going to put one in the office as president, but God has given us space to think things through and to pray it through and to get our eyes turned unto God and his righteousness, to God and his truth, to God and his mercy, to God and his love, to God and his justice, to God and his life. Hallelujah.

God doesn't want to arm murderers to rule over this nation any longer. God doesn't want to arm thieves and robbers, liars and unclean people. Hallelujah. God is God. And the nation that forgets God shall not go unpunished.

And we as a nation have got a lot to answer to God for. Gross abominations, great sins. And you want it to be business as usual? God says, NO! You're weighing in the balance, and you're found wanting. Glory to God in the highest. His will shall be done.

He says, verse four,

*Take ye heed every one of his neighbour, and trust
ye not in any brother: for every brother will utterly
supplant, and every neighbour will walk with
slanders. And they will deceive every one his
neighbour, and will not speak the truth: they have
taught their tongue to speak lies, and weary
themselves to commit iniquity.*

*Thine habitation is in the midst of deceit; through
deceit they refuse to know me, saith the LORD.*

The Lord says,

*Therefore thus saith the LORD of hosts, Behold, I
will melt them, and try them; for how shall I do for
the daughter of my people? Their tongue is as an
arrow shot out; it speaketh deceit: one speaketh
peaceably to his neighbour with his mouth, but in
heart he layeth his wait. Shall I not visit them for
these things? saith the LORD: shall not my soul be
avenged on such a nation as this?*

And he's talking about his own as well. He's talking about
the Christian that won't do right. They won't live right. That
is full of deceit and guile. They won't treat their neighbor
right. Hallelujah. Glory to God. The Christian that walks
with slander, God's speaking to us, amen.

It's time to repent and do what is right. God tells us in the
16th verse,

*I will scatter them also among the heathen, whom
neither they nor their fathers have known: and I will
send a sword after them, till I have consumed them.*

Then he says,

Thus saith the LORD of hosts, Consider ye,

The Lord is telling those who know him, consider these things, be wise, watch, don't turn your eyes, don't turn your ears, face the truth, and deal with it.

Consider ye, and call for the mourning women, that they may come; and send for cunning women,

That means wise women,

that they may come: and let them make haste, and take up a wailing for us, that our eyes may run down with tears, and our eyelids gush out with waters.

Verse 19,

For a voice of wailing is heard out of Zion, How are we spoiled! we are greatly confounded, because we have forsaken the land, because our dwellings have cast us out.

And what have we seen? Confusion, confoundness, uncertainty. Hallelujah. God is dealing, God is proving to us how sick this society is. I heard Martin Luther King say this back in the sixties, and I pondered it in my heart, but I see it so clearly. He said, this is a sick society. Well, precious Martin, if God let you look down just for a moment, you can see how sick we really are as a society.

But the Lord is on the move, God desires to heal, He desires to make whole. He is calling for true repentance. He is calling for Zion to repent. He is calling on his people.

He's calling on the preachers to repent, amen, and to lead his people into righteousness, to be a living example, not greedy, not preaching for filthy lucre's sake.

Many preachers won't go and preach the gospel unless they already have an amount of money set aside for them… they already have it placed in their minds what they want to get. And the Lord tells us to go and preach the gospel, not for filthy lucre's sake. He said the workman is worthy of his hire.

God wants his people to come back to righteousness. Many preachers are trying to outdo one another, trying to outbuild one another, trying to have greater membership than one another. This is wrong; this is competition. God didn't call us to compete with anybody.

No matter if God wants you to walk behind a mule and preach the gospel to those who are working in the field, would you do it? Jesus came lowly and meek, walking many miles, that the gospel that his Father had put in his heart may be proclaimed, training disciples.

And he's commended us to go into all the world, amen, and to gain disciples. For his name's sake, teaching disciples to observe all things whatsoever he has told us. And we're not to worry about what we're going to put on or how we're going to live, and how fair or sumptuous our lives are going to be.

It's time to quit ye like men and put on the Lord Jesus Christ. If we say we're Christians, then act like Christ Jesus. Be like Christ Jesus. Live in him. Abide in him. I tell you, we're going to answer.

And the Lord tells us in 2 Chronicles 7,

> *if my people, which are called by my name, shall humble themselves, and pray, and seek my face, and turn from their wicked ways; then will I hear from heaven, and will forgive their sin, and will heal their land.*

God will heal, he'll bring quietness, God will do it! Instead of telling people how to march and be boisterous in the streets for man, get out there and proclaim the gospel of Jesus Christ for the salvation of the souls of men. God is weighing us out. And what he sees is quite ugly, it's quite ugly.

I've been before the Lord night and day, watching and praying. Even when I wanted to turn away from the news, the Lord would tell me to look, watch, and pray. He's on the move, Christian and non-Christian alike. And it's not business as usual. God is going to have his way.

He's going to visit either with the sword or with the outpouring of the Holy Ghost. The choice is ours. What will it be? We who are called by his name. Stop your lying! Stop playing with your wives, husbands going out on the wives, and the wives going out on the husbands. Amen.

God is tired of this abomination; man, full of lust, does not know how to bring the body under subjection to the Holy Ghost. And all this filth is going on in the house of God. People of the same sex marrying one another. It's an abomination in the eyes of God. It's grossly wicked.

And even if you haven't got to that point of marrying them, even if you're lusting after them, it's an abomination in the eyes of God. And God will have the last say. And this, this vessel, God will speak through, and I will not quench the power of the Holy Ghost.

I want to be saved in the end. It's not given to the swift nor to the strong. But he that endured to the end, not by the law of the land, but by the law of the almighty God, the same shall be saved. And to God be the glory forever and ever. Hallelujah. It's time to pray.

It's time to call upon the name of the Lord. It's time to repent for the way more serious sins and for the light sins. Sin is sin. And any sin will keep us out of heaven. It's time to turn around and humble ourselves before the mighty hand of God and ask God for mercy and deliverance and redemption from our ways, from our old habits. God is looking on.

He's weighing us out, and he shall be glorified. He's made the unjust for the day of his wrath. He's made the just that we might be in his presence forevermore. What will your choice be? It's up to you. What will it be?

In the eyes of God, he desires you to be holy. In the eyes of God, he desires to love you on into glory. In the eyes of God, he desired that you might be that vessel of honor at his appearing. But the choice is yours. The choice is yours.

It's not through any other. It has to be in your own mind and your own heart. What you're going to do with Jesus Christ and with God, the Father, God, the Holy Spirit.

Will you obey him? Will you love him? Or will you reject him? Think about it. Humble your heart. Call on his name.

Amen and amen.

No Guile I

The Bible says, O taste and see that the Lord is good, and I can never, never fail to give thanks unto Him for His goodness. As long as I live, I will always be speaking of His goodness and giving Him thanks for His goodness that He has shown unto me and to all the children of men. It's by His grace, it's by His goodness that we are called by His name.

I want to go into the Word of God in St. John, the first chapter. In the very first chapter of St. John, we see Jesus bringing disciples unto Him, and two other disciples of John followed Jesus. It was beautiful how they knew that this was the one to follow.

In the very first chapter, Peter is saying in verse 34,

> *And I saw, and bare record that this is the Son of God.*

In verse 35,

> *Again the next day after John stood, and two of his disciples; and looking upon Jesus as he walked, he saith, Behold the Lamb of God! And the two disciples heard him speak, and they followed Jesus. Then Jesus turned, and saw them following, and saith unto them, What seek ye? They said unto him, Rabbi, (which is to say, being interpreted,*

This is what Jesus says of Nathanael. Nathanael had never met Jesus, but as he's coming, wondering, can anything good come out of Nazareth? Jesus, as he sees Nathanael coming… what a testimony that Jesus would say of a man that had never met him. Behold, an Israelite indeed, bless the Lord, what a testimony, in whom is no guile, no guile.

> *Nathanael saith unto him, Whence knowest thou me? Jesus answered and said unto him, Before that Philip called thee, when thou wast under the fig tree, I saw thee. Nathanael answered and saith unto him, Rabbi, thou art the Son of God; thou art the King of Israel.*

See, in the very beginning, this man perceived who Jesus is. Just a few words spoken between the two of them in their first meeting. Now we know that later on, Peter said, when Jesus asked his disciples, who do men say that I am? And they begin to say what men, what they heard people saying of Jesus Christ.

And then Jesus asked them directly, who do you say that I am? And Peter answered immediately, Thou art Christ, the son of God. That was later. But here's a man just meeting Jesus for the first time. And he hears the Lord speak of him. And he says, thou art the son of God, thou art the King of Israel.

How is he able to perceive this so suddenly, so quickly? No guile, no guile. His heart was pure, his heart was true, his heart was sincere. And as soon as he saw the truth, he knew who he was… immediately.

He didn't have to be taught of him. When Philip invited him to come and see for himself who Jesus is, can any good thing come out of Nazareth? Was Nathaniel's attitude.

But as he got up and followed Philip, he saw that not only a good thing came out of Nazareth, but out from Heaven, thou art the Son of God, thou art the King of Israel, the King!

Oh, surely an Israelite indeed. Because only those who know God, only those whose hearts are pure and seeking after God, can perceive so quickly. And this is what I want to talk about today, no guile. The Lord is coming back, looking for a church without spot or wrinkle. And no guile, no guile.

I looked up the word guile. It says crafty or deceitful, cunning, duplicity, deceit, treachery, stratagem, device, trickery, deceive, beguile, Sly. And the meaning of sly is able to do things without letting others know. Acting secretly, cunning, crafty, trickery. The word wily, using subtle tricks to deceive, crafty, cunning, sly. You see all these words run right into each other, meaning the same thing. Artful, subtle, designing, insidious. The word wile, a trick to deceive, a cunning way, ruse, a stratagem. Stratagem means a scheme or trick for deceiving an enemy, a trick, trickery.

Stratagem applies to a plan to gain one's own ends or defeat those of others by skillful deception, skillful deception. Ruse, R-U-S-E, means a scheme or device to trick or mislead others. Cunning, skill in devising or using indirect or subtle methods. Ability to mislead, trap, or escape an enemy or opponent. Slyness, craft, deceit. Deceit, the act or practice of deceiving as by falsification, concealment, or cheating. An attempt to deceive, duplicity, doubleness of heart. Thinking of scriptures? Thought, speech, or action, doubleness of heart, thought, speech, or action.

Deception by pretending to entertain one set of feelings and acting under the influence of another. That's doubleness, double-minded, the Word of God calls it. The quality or state of being double or two-fold. That's what duplicity means. It's amazing.

The Lord tells us to put on the whole armor of God that you may be able to stand against the wiles of the devil. So we know that wiles is derived from satan's character, from the devil's character. And as we, as children of men, have been born into this world by our natural parents, we have the ability to be just this, that I have described, that I have read and defined.

That's why Jesus tells us that we must be born again, that we put off the old man and his deeds, and put on the Lord Jesus Christ… The Lord Jesus Christ.

The Word of God tells us in 1 Peter, the second chapter, beginning at the 21st verse,

> *For even hereunto were ye called: because Christ also suffered for us, leaving us an example, that ye should follow his steps:*

See, this is putting on the Lord Jesus Christ. Second Peter, chapter 2, verse 21. I'll read again.

> *For even hereunto were ye called: because Christ
> also suffered for us, leaving us an example, that ye
> should follow his steps:*

Verse 22,

> *who did no sin, neither was guile found in his
> mouth:*

That's why Jesus knew Nathaniel, an Israelite indeed, one that is surely God's. Amen. Guile is a horrible thing to have, because under the disguise of guile lie lies, deceit, cunningness, craftiness, duplicity, slyness, all of these wicked things that we find in our hearts if we are not walking after God.

But how did Nathaniel, not having met Jesus, how was he able to have no guile? He was walking after God. God Almighty. He was following the law of Moses. He was going after God with his whole heart.

Remember Simeon, full of righteousness, the priest in the temple, when Jesus was brought in by Mary and Joseph and offered back to God, the Father? Simeon immediately knew who he was. Why? Because he lived a righteous life. When you walk righteously before God, these things will not have rule, these ugly and negative things will not have rule in one's heart.

To be deceitful is to be a liar. Actually, you're deceiving yourselves, first of all. You're deceiving your own self because you allowed the enemy to come in with his trickery. See in the Garden of Eden, Satan beguiled Eve.

He beguiled her. In Psalms 32, the second verse,

> *Blessed is the man unto whom the LORD imputeth not iniquity, And in whose spirit there is no guile.*

In whose spirit…You see, the spirit of man. I'm not talking about the soul right now. The writer says here in Psalms 32, verse 2,

> *Blessed is the man unto whom the LORD imputeth not iniquity, And in whose spirit there is no guile.*

You meet many Christians, many, who have been washed in the blood, who have been forgiven of their sins, who have confessed the Lord Jesus as their personal Savior. Glory to God. But their spirit is not pure.

The spirit of man is our candle. And when that spirit is defiled by sin and trickery, by the wiles of the devil, then it brings that heart into bondage because the heart is not pure before God. Remember, when Jesus taught on the Mount, the Beatitudes, Blessed are the pure in spirit, for they shall see God. They shall be called the children of God. They are gods. Amen, the pure.

The heart is to be pure, washed with the blood of Jesus Christ. But we're not stopping there. We're not stopping just by being washed. That's our first cleansing. The Word of God continues to clean, it continues to purify. It continues to purge. This is why we must stay in the law of the Lord.

We must stay in the Word of God, day and night, that we might learn who Jesus is. He said, take my yoke upon you and learn of me. Many times, Jesus and the Father are abused by the way that His children use Him.

Amen. They take His love for granted and they abuse that precious love. Oh, God knows my heart. That's the problem. He knows what's in the heart. When He saw Nathaniel, He knew what was in Nathaniel's heart.

And not once do we see as Nathaniel walked with the other disciples, where Jesus had to reprove him firsthand. Amen. But we saw him get Peter, because Peter had other things on his mind. He was double-minded. You see, he had not learned how to walk with Jesus like many today.

But we can… we can learn. We can listen to those that God has anointed. And we can listen mainly to the Anointed One, the Holy Ghost, the Spirit of Truth. He will lead us and guide us into all truth. And one thing about Him, He will search the intents of our hearts before God, our Maker. Deep calleth unto the deep.

The soul of man is deep. And that soul wants its Maker. It wants right standing with God Almighty. And the spirit of man has to come under also the subjection of God, the authority of God, the power of God, in order to be pure. Many things are in the spirit. We hear people saying, oh, you're hurting, you're hurting.

Many times you're hurting because it's something embedded in the spirit, in your spirit, that you have not allowed God to deal with. And God has called us to wellness, wellness of mind, healthy minds, healthy spirits, healthy souls, not just healthy bodies.

Jesus paid it all so that we would be completely made whole in His sight. So I want you to listen very closely to what the Lord is saying to us today. When God saw Nathaniel, God the Son, saw this man sitting up under fig tree, and He told him, I saw thee.

Here's what the Lord said to him. And this is marvelous. When Jesus answered in verse 50, of St. John 1,

> *Jesus answered and said unto him, Because I said unto thee, I saw thee under the fig tree, believest thou? thou shalt see greater things than these.*

You shall see greater things than these!

> *And he saith unto him, Verily, verily, I say unto you, Hereafter ye shall see heaven open, and the angels of God ascending and descending upon the Son of man.*

Why? No guile, visions, seeing the Lord walking in His rightful place, dear children of God. This is our rightful place to know the things that pertain to heaven. Hallelujah. To be able to discern, to be able to see, to be able to perceive heavenly things!

This is what Jesus said to this man in their first meeting. Isn't this marvelous? Let me read this again. Verse 49,

> *Nathanael answered and saith unto him, Rabbi, thou art the Son of God; thou art the King of Israel.*

> *Jesus answered and said unto him, Because I said unto thee, I saw thee under the fig tree, believest thou? thou shalt see greater things than these.*

Greater. In other words, I told you, I saw you under the fig tree, even before Philip came and got you. I saw you sitting there, hallelujah, at a distance.

And he told Nathanael, Nathanael gets excited. And because he gets excited that the Lord saw him afar off. He perceived by the power of God that this is indeed the Son of God, the Christ, the Messiah, the King of Israel.

> *And he saith unto him, Verily, verily, I say unto you, Hereafter ye shall see heaven open,*

Now, the word of God tells us in the writings of Paul, the eye hath not seen, nor the ear heard the good things that the Lord hath in store for them that love him, but they are revealed unto us by his Spirit. His Spirit.

And this is what the Lord was telling Nathanael, because your heart is guileless. You're not crafty and deceitful and full of lies and hypocrisies, because that's what it boils down to. Hallelujah.

What a beautiful relationship. But God has ordained this relationship, this kind of relationship and commands this relationship for every one of us, no guile, spotless, blameless at his appearing. So it's an everyday walk. You know what it's called? Holiness… Holiness.

Living clean, being pure and righteous in the eyes of God, that he might reveal himself, that these good things that he has in store, like he's telling Nathanael, might be revealed unto us.

He has no respect of persons… Whosoever will, and Nathanael came, didn't he? Jesus said, whosoever will, let them come and drink of the water of life freely. And here is the promise.

> *Verily, verily, I say unto you, Hereafter ye shall see heaven open, and the angels of God ascending and descending upon the Son of man.*

Hallelujah. Ministering unto Jesus Christ, you shall behold this, Nathanael, because you are guileless and you believe. You believe… You see, when guile is taken away, faith comes forth, and you are able to see those things that God wants you to see. This is our walk that God promised us on this side of Heaven.

What? Know you not that the kingdom of heaven is within you and you are not your own? That's what Paul asked. Don't you know that you belong to God? Blessed is the man unto whom the Lord imputed not iniquity and in whose spirit there is no guile.

It can be done. It can be done, and it shall be done. It must be done. It's the command of God. Jesus said, now you're clean through the word which I have spoken unto you. And as we continue to eat the word of God, the bread that he has given unto us to eat daily, you're purified more and more, made clean.

Clean in spirit, clean, pure in heart, the mind clear, the eyes anointed to see those glorious things that only heaven can reveal by God's Holy Spirit. For even hereunto were you called because Christ also suffered for us, leaving us an example that you should follow his steps who did no sin, neither was guile found in his mouth.

Revelation 14 verse 5 says,

> *And in their mouth was found no guile: for they are without fault before the throne of God.*

Meaning those who had surrendered their lives to Jesus Christ and knew not woman.

God is moving by his spirit. He's purifying the church of Jesus Christ worldwide. It's time for us to allow in all honesty and truthfulness for the Holy Ghost to have his way in our hearts and let him search the things that are contrary to the will of God.

God be with you till we meet again. Amen.

No Guile II

First Aired Feb 28th, 1999

We thank God for the opportunity again to be with you in the name of Jesus. And we count it a victory to be here in the name of Jesus, bless His holy name.

Last week we spoke to you concerning No Guile, and we shall continue on this subject, No Guile. But before we go any further, we ask you to bow with us in prayer. In the precious name of Jesus, Father, we come before your throne of grace.

We thank you for this title, this subject, No Guile. We thank you for all the word of God, for it is a lamp unto our feet and a light unto our pathway. We know, Lord, by your Spirit, you are getting us ready to meet Jesus in the air.

And we thank you for your engrafted word. We thank you for the hidden riches that are in your word, and they are brought forth unto us. They are revealed unto us by your spirit.

We thank you for the revelation knowledge of Jesus Christ. We thank you for the work and the ministry of the Holy Ghost in this earth. We know, and always will know, that you are here to prepare us to meet Jesus, Holy Spirit of God.

Help us to be willing to be led by your Holy Spirit, Father, that we will not grieve Him, but give Him our utmost attention and willingness of heart, mind, soul, and spirit.

That we might be obedient to your Holy Spirit that you've given to us freely, to lead us and guide us into all truth, and to present us blameless, thoughtless at your appearing. As we go into the Word, enlighten our eyes and open our ears, soften and melt our hearts.

If you find anything, Father, in us that is displeasing in your sight, correct it with thy mighty, powerful word. Help us to be yielded at all times. Help us to be children in heart, willing to be corrected. Bind the forces of hell that would seek to destroy the word of God in us.

Satan, the Lord rebuke you. I plead the blood of Jesus against you right now. I usurp the authority of Jesus Christ over all your evil works, and I command the will of the Lord to be done in each heart.

Thy will be done, thy kingdom come, you taught us to pray. On earth, that means in our earthly vessels as well, as it is in heaven, as your holy angels are obeying you in heaven. Accomplish your divine purpose in us. The plan that you've already set for our lives helps us to follow therein with fullness of heart and complete subjection to the will of the most high God.

Thy will be done. Watch upon your word, send it forth under the unction and the anointing of the Holy Ghost. Pierce the darkness that he would find in any heart right now. Praise your glorious name.

Turn with me again to St. John, the first chapter, verse 43,

> *The day following Jesus would go forth into*
> *Galilee, and findeth Philip, and saith unto*

him, Follow me. Now Philip was of Bethsaida, the city of Andrew and Peter.

Philip findeth Nathanael, and saith unto him, We have found him, of whom Moses in the law, and the prophets, did write, Jesus of Nazareth, the son of Joseph. And Nathanael said unto him, Can there any good thing come out of Nazareth? Philip saith unto him, Come and see.

Come and see…

Jesus saw Nathanael coming to him, and saith of him, Behold an Israelite indeed, in whom is no guile!

I'm reminded of the word of God, where it tells us it's not the circumcision… that will not profit anything; it's done away with. In the eyes of God, we are not clean through circumcision or uncircumcision. We're clean from the heart, not the foreskin, but the heart, the heart of man. It's the heart that God is looking on. God sees and knows our hearts.

He knows our thoughts before they can enter the heart. But he says of Philip, an Israelite indeed in whom is no guile, to really be of the city of God, we must have no guile, every one of us.

It's amazing that out of all the 12 disciples that Jesus called to follow him, he said of only one at the first meeting, and that was to Nathaniel, an Israelite indeed in whom is no guile. Nathaniel lived after God. Listen, as we read on,

I saw thee. Before you came, before Philip even came to
you, I saw you under the fig tree. So, God's eyes are upon
us, the children of men. His eyes are beholding the children
of men. Whether we are Christians or not, whether we are
children of God or not, God knows us.

Now, one might ask oneself, what can be greater than
knowing that Jesus Christ is surely God, the Son, or the
Son of God, the king of Israel? To have that knowledge, to
have that understanding, what could be greater? Jesus said,

The Son of man, ascending and descending upon the Son of
man.

You shall see heaven open. God is granting Nathaniel the privilege because he is an Israelite indeed. There's no guile in him, no deceit in him.

He is granting him the privilege to see the angels of the Lord coming down to Jesus Christ. And then the angels ascending back from Jesus Christ back to heaven, seeing heaven doors open. This is what God promised Nathaniel in Nathaniel's day, while Nathaniel was still upon the earth at their first meeting.

Nathaniel perceives, because there's no guile in him to block his sight, Nathaniel perceives that this indeed is not one that is called a Nazarite; He's God's Son. He's not just from Nazareth, He's not the son of Joseph, He's the king of Israel. And he perceives this right on their first meeting. Marvelous... And the Lord said, you shall see greater things than these.

Greater because his eyes are open, his heart is yielded, his spirit is pure, he's clean. Living clean, sitting up under that big tree. Glory to God in the highest!

God is looking for vessels today just like Nathaniel. It was God who made Nathaniel that way. And because he was made that way, he was able to immediately perceive who Jesus is. Many people spend a lifetime on the face of this earth, and yet they're saying, is there really a God? And some will say, oh, there's no God. We are our own gods. I am my own God.

Very foolish. The word of God say, you say you're gods, you say, well, but you shall die like men. That's what the word says. And to die like men can be an awesome, horrible death outside of Jesus Christ, who is that way, the only way. Amen.

So we see how important it is to have no guile. I read the definitions in the last broadcast concerning guile. It means crafty or deceitful cunning. Duplicity, deceit, treachery. Stratagem, device. Beguile, deceive, sly, able to do things without letting others know. Acting secretly, cunning, crafty, trickery. Wildly, using subtle tricks to deceive.

Artful, subtle, designing, insidious. A trick to deceive. That's what wild means. A cunning way. Ruse, again, stratagem. Stratagem means a scheme or trick for deceiving an enemy: a trick, trickery. Stratagem applies to a plan to gain one's own ends or defeat those of others by skillful deception. Ruse means a scheme or device to trick or mislead others, and one word goes into another. Cunning, duplicity, deceive, and so forth.

This, none of this, none of this subtle work of that old serpent called the devil was found in Nathanael. None. Glory to God in the highest. And God would have us to be the same way. I'll read to you, in Ephesians, yes, in Ephesians, the fifth chapter. It talks about the husbands and the wives loving one another and submitting ourselves one to another in the fear of God. But then we see earlier how the Lord likens his union with us as one that is married to his wife.

We won't go into that because there's not time. Maybe at another date. But he says in verse 25,

> *Husbands, love your wives, even as Christ also loved the church, and gave himself for it;*

And this is the reason why He gave himself for the church,

> *that he might sanctify and cleanse it with the washing of water by the word,*

By the word. This is how we see ourselves. This is our mirror. Naturally, we go to a glass mirror, and we look into it to see how we are. So we go spiritually into the word of God, which is the mirror of our souls. It tells us the will of God for our lives.

And this is what the word will do. Jesus said in St. John 15, now you're clean, clean through the word which I've spoken unto you. And the apostle Paul picks it up, and he says, verse 26, that he might sanctify and cleanse it.

First, he sets us apart, and then he continues his cleansing grace with the washing of water by the word. And this is why there are three that bear witness in the earth, as well as three that bear witness in heaven. The water, the word, the spirit bears witness on earth, washing us, purifying our hearts and our spirits, sanctifying our minds.

That's the work of the Holy Spirit. This is why he is here. He's gathering us together to purify and cleanse the church, the body of Christ. He calls us the bride. The bridegroom is coming, and the Holy Spirit is stepping up his pace in cleansing and purifying that the church might be pure.

The church has fallen far away from the perfect plan of God. It's not operating in the fullness of God's power. It's not operating in the knowledge of who Jesus is. Some cannot get farther than salvation, but we've got to get past salvation. We've got to see as the Lord promised Nathaniel.

We've got to see what God has in store for us here. This world is full of corruption. It's full of guile. You name it, it's here. And Satan is letting out more demons out of that fiery pit daily to deceive and beguile the Christian and the world as a whole.

But the Lord is saying that he is also here to keep us separated from this evil world. And the allurements of this world. Glory to God. We see by Nathaniel being able to perceive who Jesus is that the world didn't have anything to offer him. He stayed free in spirit. He stayed pure in heart. Hallelujah.

Jesus said, in whom is no guile, no deceit, no lie, no hypocrisy. None of this abominable stuff that the devil can throw at us. Amen. I'm sure he came after Nathaniel. But Nathaniel rejected him. He resisted him by submitting himself to that which he knew of God. And therefore, being a prayerful man, he had to be. When he saw God the Son, he said, you are the Son of God, the King of Israel, right off.

So that means he knew the word; he knew that God was going to send his Son. And he also knew that he would be the King of Israel. And Nathaniel, he's King of all the earth.

And one day, he shall take his rightful place in this world. Hallelujah. He's going to rule this world. He's coming back to rule this world. But in the meantime, he's getting his body in order. We are his body. Praise God.

Now look what he says,

> that he might present it to himself a glorious church,

Not a church that is without the goodness of God. Not a church that is trying to do her best to stay right. No, that's not good enough. The Holy Ghost is here to help us to be right with God.

> *that he might present it to himself a glorious church, not having spot, or wrinkle, or any such thing;*

Any such thing, anything that will defile us… Free of it, freedom from sin. You mean to tell me you got the nerve to say that we can be without sin? No guile, no sin.

Washed in the blood and not willfully committing the sin, running to God, and saying, Lord, forgive me, I sinned. But if I sin again, I know you're going to forgive me. That's premeditated sinning. Presumptuous and self-willed. No, no, there's a better plan.

And God will see to it by his Spirit that we measure up to God's divine purpose and plan for his church. We're not going out of here full of sin or not even a spot that is sinful. Bless his holy name.

Believe it or not, we're to take the word of God literally. This is not just a book of poetry. I got news for you.

This is the word of God. And we're to live by it night and day, 24 hours every day until Jesus comes,

> *that he might present it to himself a glorious church, not having spot, or wrinkle, or any such thing; but that it should be holy and without blemish.*

And you say, well, Jesus is all of that in my life. But Jesus has called us to be also holy, holy and without blame, without sin.

In 2 Peter, the third chapter, he writes,

> *This second epistle, beloved, I now write unto you; in both which I stir up your pure minds by way of remembrance:*

In other words, I'm bringing you to remembrance

> *that ye may be mindful of the words which were spoken before by the holy prophets, and of the commandment of us the apostles of the Lord and Saviour: knowing this first, that there shall come in the last days scoffers, walking after their own lusts, and saying, Where is the promise of his coming? for since the fathers fell asleep, all things continue as they were from the beginning of the creation.*

> *For this they willingly are ignorant of,*

They are willing to be ignorant of God's will.

For this they willingly are ignorant of, that by the word of God the heavens were of old, and the earth standing out of the water and in the water: whereby the world that then was, being overflowed with water, perished: but the heavens and the earth, which are now, by the same word are kept in store, reserved unto fire against the day of judgment and perdition of ungodly men.

But beloved, be not ignorant of this one thing, that one day is with the Lord as a thousand years and a thousand years as one day. The Lord is not slack concerning his promise, as some men count slackness, but is long suffering to us, Lord, not willing that any should perish, but that all should come to repentance.

But the day of the Lord will come as a thief in the night; in the which the heavens shall pass away with a great noise, and the elements shall melt with fervent heat,

The earth also and the works that are therein shall be burned up. This is what is coming on the face of this earth.

Seeing then that all these things shall be dissolved, what manner of persons ought ye to be in all holy conversation and godliness,

Seeing that this earth is going down, the stars and the moon and the sun are going down. Everything that God said will go down; it's going down. But the word of God and those who are established in the word, those who have made the

Lord their trust, and have desired and willed to obey the word of God.

The word is what's going to bring us home at peace with God. The word in us as we are keepers and doers of his word. Some will hide the word; they'll know the word, but they won't do it.

God is saying be doers of the word, not hearers only. Just don't pack it in the head and not allow it to come and flow in the heart and saturate your very being. We're to live by God's word every day. And Jesus told us to pray for that daily bread. Praise his holy name.

> Seeing then that all these things shall be dissolved, what manner of persons ought ye to be in all holy conversation and godliness,

We're to walk godly. That means like God on this earth, like Him. How do we walk like him? Living in him and He in us. That's how we walk, and then obeying him.

> *Nevertheless we, according to his promise, look for new heavens and a new earth, wherein dwelleth righteousness.*
>
> *Wherefore, beloved, seeing that ye look for such things, be diligent that ye may be found of him in peace, without spot, and blameless.*

He tells us to look diligently within ourselves according to God's word that we might be found without spot when Jesus comes, blameless. That's our responsibility to our own souls and for our own souls. Let's obey God.

I know Jesus is coming soon, and you know. Obey God in
his precious name. God be with you.

Amen and amen.

No Guile III

First Aired March 7th, 1999

Precious greetings to every one of you in the name of the Lord and Savior Jesus Christ. We thank God for enabling us to be with you again, and it's my utmost desire that you've been following with us, especially these last two Sundays. We have been ministering on the subject, no guile, no guile.

I thank God for enabling me to bring these words to you from the Word of God. It is so important because we are in the last hour of the last days. I truly believe this with all my heart, and Jesus has told us, precious ones, that we are to be holy, even as our Father in heaven is holy.

That means everything, our conduct, our thoughts, even what we would plan, our interaction with one another, knowing who we are for our own sakes, what God has made us to be because we are blood-washed, we've been born again.

I'm speaking to the Christian today, and I suppose you would say I speak to the Christians every time you're here, and that's true. My ministry is mainly to God's people, but it's amazing, and I'm always surprised, many times by the letters that I get, especially from abroad, telling me how just listening to the ministry of Praise, Power, and Prayer Temple, God's Holy Mountain broadcast, how they're saved, they're challenged to get to know God for themselves, and how many Christians write me and tell me how they are determined to follow on to know the Lord Jesus Christ as I am ministering His Word.

So, I thank God for this privilege and for the opportunity to share what the Holy Spirit shares with me. God is good, and we know because of His goodness, He is not willing that any man would be corrupt and full of guile. You thought I was going to say not willing that any man perish.

Well, that's fact, because if we are corrupt and full of guile or any guile, we shall perish if Jesus were to come immediately. We ought to hear the voice of God, no matter who He uses. The Word of God is right.

The Word of God is true, and God is concerned about the way we live in this present world. We carry His name. His name represents goodness. It represents good and love, mercy, truth, equity, justice, and so forth. God is so good, and Jesus says of those who belong to God that our fruit is good. We should therefore bring forth fruit, and our fruit that we bring forth unto God, it should remain the fruit of righteousness, love, honesty, truth.

Anything that is good and wholesome is of God. We, in our endemic nature… we're not good. God looked for someone on the face of this earth, and everyone failed in one sense or another.

So, therefore, God sent His only begotten Son, Jesus Christ, that He might redeem the world…the world. Whosoever would believe on Him, it is His desire to redeem. No matter what the sin or the failure might be, corruption, you name it, it's found in mankind worldwide.

It doesn't matter what nation we are from or the nationality
we are of; man is prone to sin. We are of a fallen nature…
Adam and Eve. And Jesus said that we must be born again,
and if we are born again, He said, all things are passed
away, and behold, all things are become new. He spoke that
through the Apostle Paul.

Our minds are made new. Our hearts are made anew. What
we took pleasure in through sinning, we no longer desire,
and we should remain that way. But also the Word of God
tells us in the sixth chapter of Ephesians that we are to put
on the whole armor of God, because when we are
redeemed, when the Lord saves us from our sins, there is an
opponent. His name is called the devil. He is also called the
destroyer. He's the one who is full of corruption and guile.
He's full of it, and He is the one who has planted corruption
and guile in the hearts and minds of people, of individuals.

So, when He loses us through our turning unto Jesus and
the Lord washing us from our sins with His own blood that
He shed for our sins, the devil has desired to set out to
destroy us, to trip us up, to cause us to fail in one form or
another. And this is why the Word of God tells us to put on
the whole armor of God, that we might be able to withstand
the devil, to withstand his wiles that he would bring against
us through subtlety.

I'm still ministering on this subject, no guile, no guile. And
I've read to you the definition of guile. I'll read one or two
definitions here again.

It means crafty or deceitful, cunning, duplicity, treachery, device, trickery, beguile, and to deceive, deception. This is what He did to Eve in the Garden of Eden. And He has not stopped there. He conquered her and Adam and caused them to fall from the grace of God. And He is still carrying out His wiles today against humanity.

But we are to live above what goes on in the world. We're to live unto Jesus Christ while yet here in this world. We're to live a holy life, a life that represents Jesus Christ. He lives in us, and we are to allow Him to have His way in us and through us. We are to be obedient people of God. That's what discipleship is all about, being disciplined in our walk with Jesus Christ, with Jesus Christ. Hallelujah.

This is why, as I sought the Lord many years ago, back in the early 80s, that's how long I've been broadcasting in different parts of the world. The Lord gave me the name God's Holy Mountain Broadcast to give us to know that there's a higher walk for us Christians while we are yet in this present world. We are not to accept the devil's definition of what a Christian is like.

We're to accept the Word of God as to what we are and what we should be. Glory to God. We are to live and walk a high-standing walk. We're to walk this high and lofty way. And as the Lord said of Nathaniel, He should be able to say concerning everyone that name His name, everyone that says we are born again, the Lord should say of us all, in whose spirit there is no guile. He said it of Nathaniel; he should be able to quickly say it of every one of us.

But that's not always the case, and this is why we have the epistles found in the Word of God, the gospels and the epistles, and also the book of Revelation, to warn us not to fall in Satan's deceptions, not to live as carnal Christians in the flesh and not walking after the Holy Spirit, who is here to lead us and guide us into all truth and to cause us to live a victorious life. So from the scriptures, I would like to show you what the Lord says. It's found in Psalms 101.

> *I will sing of mercy and judgment: Unto thee,*
> *O LORD, will I sing. I will behave myself wisely In*
> *a perfect way. O when wilt thou come unto me? I*
> *will walk within my house with a perfect heart.*

And that's what God tells us to do, be perfect. That means mature, grow in his grace, grow in the knowledge of who he is, and live accordingly. Perfect house, that means in our clay tabernacle, our house of clay, the Lord abides. He said,

> *I will set no wicked thing before mine eyes: I hate*
> *the work of them that turn aside; It shall not cleave*
> *to me. A froward heart shall depart from me: I will*
> *not know a wicked person.*

In other words, I will not be in the company and do things constantly with a wicked person. I will not be partners in wickedness.

> *Whoso privily slandereth his neighbour, Him will I*
> *cut off: Him that hath an high look And a proud*
> *heart will not I suffer. Mine eyes shall be upon the*
> *faithful Of the land, that they may dwell with me:*

Faithful to be obedient to the will of God, to the word of God. And it should be hidden in our hearts that when temptation comes, we will not fall snare to the fowler or to the deceiver who is the devil. We are to be faithful to the word of God in us.

> *He that walketh in a perfect way, He shall serve me.*

You see God's definition of servants? He that walketh in a perfect way, the person that walks according to the word of God, rightly divided, that is, they shall serve him.

> *He that worketh deceit shall not dwell within my house: He that telleth lies shall not tarry in my sight.*

Let me read this again.

> *He that worketh deceit shall not dwell within my house:*

That means doing deceitful things. Deceitfulness, when it all boils down to it, guile, is nothing but lies. And deceit, lies, and deception, guile, full of hypocrisy, guile, lies, not only telling them, but also believing them. And the word of God tells us in Revelation that what it is, what the results of that person will be, that telleth and believeth a lie.

So it is important for us to see to it that our souls and our hearts and our minds are not engulfed in deceit of any kind, without or within, because the devil is a big lie. Jesus said he is the father of lies because he's a liar from the beginning. And whatsoever he deceives you in, it's to deceive you to lie, to believe a lie.

So remember, guile is cunning craftiness, and it describes Satan for what he really is. It's deceit, all kinds of wily devices to cause others to believe a lie. And the word duplicity means doubleness of heart, thought, speech, or action. Doubleness of heart, thought, speech, or action.

We look at the world system, and we desire to see righteousness. And we hear lies and deception all over the place. Governments of nations built on lies and empty promises because they are not following after God Almighty. Oh, they may boast of him. They quote scriptures. They may say they know him, but Jesus said, you shall know them by their fruit.

If a liar speaks lies, then we know that they are not of God Almighty because he is truth, truth. And the Lord said he desires truth in the inward parts. In the innermost being, he desires truth. He doesn't want us to be sly and full of craftiness to do harm or evil or falsehood against ourselves or against one another. That is not the love of God. And we are to love.

That is the commandment that Jesus Christ gave us: to love God and to love one another. He said, A new commandment I give unto you that you love one another. And if you love one another, you don't want to deceive one another. It's not in your heart to do anything ill against another, whether they belong to God or not.

We are to live honestly before a darkened and evil world. Honestly, not in craftiness, nor deceit, nor lies.

The Bible tells us to lie not one to another, seeing that you have put off the old man and his deeds. That's found in Colossians, the third chapter, ninth verse. Lie not one to another. That's guile… guile.

And we wonder why God will not speak. We wonder why God will not make Himself known. Search the heart. Search the heart. What does God find there? Now let me read Psalms 101, verses seven and eight again.

> *He that worketh deceit shall not dwell within my house: He that telleth lies shall not tarry in my sight.*

Tarry means to wait before God. Then the Psalmist says in another part, if I regard iniquity in my heart, the Lord shall not hear me. You want God to hear you? You want to get a prayer through quickly? Walk with God in all honesty. Walk with him in truth. Walk with him, no matter what the devil comes and brings against you.

Walk in truth, walk honestly before God and humanity. Now, evil people, no matter how honest you are, will never see honesty. They will never see pureness. They only see what they know in their own hearts. But as long as you know through the word, through the written word, through the living word, that your heart is right and pure, then God calls you holy, and he will hear you. He will allow you to wait in his presence.

Wait on him until he answers.

He that worketh deceit shall not dwell within my house: He that telleth lies shall not tarry in my sight. I will early destroy all the wicked of the land;

That day is coming

That I may cut off All wicked doers from the city of the LORD.

New Jerusalem will have no wicked person abiding within its walls. Glory to God. No person who has any guile whatsoever. We know that Jesus, the word of God, says in 1 Peter, the second chapter, verse 21st,

For even hereunto were ye called: because Christ also suffered for us, leaving us an example, that ye should follow his steps:

Verse 22,

who did no sin,

We are to follow the steps of Jesus. He is our perfect example. God did not send any person who was flawed to be our example. He sent the perfect one, and he proved faithful to the very end, to the very end of his life on this earth.

who did no sin, neither was guile found in his mouth:

Speaking of Jesus, who did no sin, neither was guile found in his mouth. And this is how we are to walk. He is that perfect example.

And we are to walk, not just after him, but in him. Choosing what God is, above what self the world of the devil desires. We are to choose what God is. What God is, is holy. What God is, is pure. What God is, is truth. He's true. His nature, his characteristics are truthfulness. In him is no guile.

And in those that are born again, there is no guile. When we walk with him, there is no guile. We have not learned Jesus Christ in any other form, except pureness, except beautiful perfection, except the beauties of holiness.

This is what we see in Jesus Christ. No matter what we look at in the scriptures concerning him, we see pureness. We see love. We see love unfamed. We see the knowledge of God. We see the wisdom of God. We see the pureness of God. And that's why the word of God, the psalmist tells us, oh taste and see that the Lord is good. He is good! He's full of goodness. And his children are also.

He's a compassionate God. He's a merciful God. And his children are also. We don't want to be numbered as good workers, faithful workers, and yet liars and deceivers. Amen. I'm not talking about being branded by man, I'm talking about God, his testimony towards us, what he sees, what he knows.

Praise his holy name. We want to dwell with him while we yet live on the face of this earth. We want to dwell and walk this high and lofty way that God has already planned for us.

He's high, and he's holy. And we are to walk through the blood of Jesus Christ, through the knowledge of who God is. Praise his holy name.

This is what we call communion with God. When he said, I will come in, if we open up the doors of our heart and let him come in, he said, I will sup with you and you with me. And so it's a twofold thing.

We don't take God's love and his provisions for our lives to be pure for granted. We are to fellowship with him, and we are to walk as Jesus walked when he was here. He's walking in us by his spirit, but let us be doers of his word and not hearers only. Praise his holy name. In the book of Isaiah, the word of God says, in chapter 53, verse 9, speaking of Jesus,

> *And he made his grave with the wicked, and with the rich in his death; because he had done no violence, neither was any deceit in his mouth.*

Neither was any deceit in his mouth. So his life was spotless all the way through. Now, the scribes and the Pharisees and those who hated Jesus Christ, they branded him a liar from the beginning. They said he was a bastard. He was born a bastard. They said all kinds of wicked things about the Son of the living God who came down from heaven to redeem us.

And many are saying the same thing of him today. They said he was a thief because he was trying to make himself equal with God. They called him a murderer.

They called him all kinds of things. They called him the chief of devils, Beelzebub, because they did not understand the power of God in operation. Praise the Lord of hosts.

When he spoke in other tongues to bring deliverance to the damsel that was dead, they laughed him to scorn, or they tried to until he put them all out. Jesus was full of purity. There is no guile in him, not even today. There is no guile.

And as we grow in his grace and in the knowledge of who he is, there should be no guile found in his children. We are called to walk with Jesus Christ, the hope of glory, by pureness, by knowledge, by love, unfeigned towards all mankind and especially the household of faith.

Do not work deceit against one another. God is not pleased. God has given us life abundantly. Let's live it to the fullness, to live pure and holy and righteous in our spirits while there's still a little time left. God be with you is our utmost desire as you seek his holy face, call on his name night and day until you know Jesus.

The Lord Our Confidence I

First Aired Feb 7th, 1999

Greetings, everyone. We thank God for being here today. We always thank God for His goodness and His mercies to bring us unto His holy will. And we thank the Lord for the privilege of coming your way today by the way of radio. We thank God for what He is doing in the earth. God is so good to us and merciful.

He's kind and generous and long-suffering towards us, the children of men. And for this cause, we give Him praise. Thank God for His goodness. We thank God for Jesus Christ, who has made all of this that we have experienced and we have access to in the kingdom of God. Jesus Christ made all of this possible; it's Jesus.

As the songwriter says, Oh, it is Jesus, and surely it is, that gave His life a ransom for us, that we could be counted worthy to come into the presence of God in Jesus' name. Thank you, Jesus. Let us pray.

Holy Father, we thank You for Your loving kindness and Your tender mercies and all that You've shown unto us down through the years. Even those who have just been saved, Lord, thank You for the privilege of knowing You in the pardon of our sins and giving us Your Son, Jesus, to be our Savior. Amen.

We give You praise, and we give You honor. Now bring forth Your Word today. Lord, these are troublesome times in which we are living.

But we know that You are God and You're yet ruling on Your throne. And we're asking today that Your Word will come forth under the auction and the power of the Holy Ghost. We need to hear from You, Lord.

We need to be encouraged. Many are going through trials and tribulations. Many have been tested on every side. Many, Lord God, would have given up had it not been for the power of Your Word. Encouraging the heart to stand and go through. We thank You for the Word of God.

We thank You for the ministry of the Holy Ghost. Take charge, Holy Spirit, right now. Give the utterance and enlighten our eyes. Encourage our hearts. Show us the way that we must take. Glory to God.

Manifest the Word of God unto us. In Jesus' name. And bind the forces of hell that will come to steal and to rob from us. Give the children of God to stand up in faith and believe and trust the living God. Your Word is Your testimony unto us, the children of men. And You've given it freely, Lord, that anyone who desires can look into the perfect law of liberty and be made free.

Thy will be done. Thy kingdom come. In Jesus' name. Amen. Psalms 118 and also Psalms 10. The psalmist in chapter 10 of the book of Psalms, David, says,

> *Why standest thou afar off, O LORD? Why hidest thou thyself in times of trouble?*

Sometimes it seems that way. But we know that God is not afar off. When David wrote this, David didn't have the knowledge that we have today. We have Jesus Christ.

And Jesus said, I will never leave you nor forsake you. But sometimes when the heart and the soul are going through deep and bitter trials, it feels like God is afar off. And so it's good for the soul to cry out unto God no matter what.

> *Why standest thou afar off, O LORD?*
>
> *Why hidest thou thyself in times of trouble?*
>
> *The wicked in his pride doth persecute the poor:*
>
> *Let them be taken in the devices that they have imagined.*
>
> *For the wicked boasteth of his heart's desire,*
>
> *And blesseth the covetous, whom the LORD abhorreth.*
>
> *The wicked, through the pride of his countenance, will not seek after God:*
>
> *God is not in all his thoughts.*
>
> *His ways are always grievous; Thy judgments are far above out of his sight:*
>
> *As for all his enemies, he puffeth at them.*

This is the heart of the wicked. They think they can get away with anything and everything.

> *He hath said in his heart, I shall not be moved:*

For I shall never be in adversity.

You see, they have believed the lies of their father, the devil.

His mouth is full of cursing and deceit and fraud:

Under his tongue is mischief and vanity.

He sitteth in the lurking places of the villages:

In the secret places doth he murder the innocent:
His eyes are privily set against the poor.

He lieth in wait secretly as a lion in his den:

He lieth in wait to catch the poor:

He doth catch the poor, when he draweth him into his net.

He croucheth, and humbleth himself,

That the poor may fall by his strong ones.

He hath said in his heart, God hath forgotten:

He hideth his face; he will never see it.

Arise, O LORD; O God, lift up thine hand:

Forget not the humble.

Wherefore doth the wicked contemn God?

He hath said in his heart, Thou wilt not require it.

David is gathering strength now, and he has seen God as
God is.

Psalms 118,

God will not forsake his own. He's ever merciful. He's ever
tender in mercy, and he's full of love, and he is watching
over his own.

Let Israel now say,

That his mercy endureth for ever.

Let the house of Aaron now say,

That his mercy endureth for ever.

Let them now that fear the LORD say,

That his mercy endureth for ever.

called upon the LORD in distress:

See, like in Psalms 10.

> The LORD answered me, *and set me* in a large
> place.

> The LORD *is* on my side;

God proved himself. When God's children begin to pray
and pour out their soul unto God, even in distress, God
hears, and God will answer. He said,

> *I called upon the LORD in distress:*

> *The LORD answered me, and set me in a large
> place.*

> *The LORD is on my side;*

> *I will not fear: What can man do unto me?*

Hallelujah!

> *The LORD taketh my part with them that help me:*

What is my desire upon them that hate me? My desires, Lord, do not allow those who hate my soul see their desire upon me. Amen, for you have favored my righteous cause. Glory be to God.

It is better to trust in the LORD

Than to put confidence in man.

It is better to trust in the LORD

Than to put confidence in princes.

See, Jesus did not submit himself to man; He submitted himself to the Father because he knew what was in the heart of man. Glory to God. And this is how God wants us to be. He wants us to be loving. He wants us to be kind. He wants us to be friendly, and he wants us to be a friend. But our confidence is in God. He is the maker of our souls. And God is our defense. God can not fail us. God will not fail us.

It is the will of the Lord to show his marvelous strength and his loving kindness. God loves it when we put our trust in him. For he says, there is one who believes in me, I can manifest myself to that one. God loves faith. Amen, Hallelujah. The psalmist says,

All nations compassed me about:

But in the name of the LORD will I destroy them.

How? How will I destroy all nations? Because I believe in the word of God. I am no longer saying, why are you standing afar off? Why won't you answer? But God has shown himself to me. This is what David is saying.

And God has proven that he is with me. So I shall not fear man. I will fear God. I will put my trust in God. And in the name of the Lord, anything that would arise against me, I am going to quench it with the power of God's word. With the power to pray and with the power and confidence in God's word, I shall destroy anything that rises against me. Didn't Jesus say that? Jesus said, behold, I give you power over all devils. Amen.

I believe God. I believe that there is no power except it be ordained of God. I believe that anything that comes against us, God has allowed it that he might show himself mighty on our behalf. I believe that every trial and every test God allows to come our way is for our coming unto God and learning who our God is.

Jesus said, take my yoke upon you and learn of me. Amen. He is the most excellent one. He is the power and the authority and the wisdom and the knowledge. He is our faith. And there is no failure in God.

These are testing times for Christians around the world. Many, as I've aforestated, many have given up their lives that we are not even hearing about in this nation of ours. But many Christians coming from the religious front, the religious news, news behind the news, we're finding out many are being martyred because they believe on the Lord Jesus Christ.

Even little children. Many lives are being destroyed, but the soul is still intact. Satan can never destroy the church of Jesus Christ. He may fight against us, and he may kill some, but he cannot destroy the church of the living God. The Lord is on our side. And no matter who's ruling in the nations, God is still on the side of his children.

Jesus has already told us in the word of God that many would give up their lives for his sake. Bless his holy name. And this is why we are not to fear anyone who can kill our bodies.

Jesus said, do not fear the one who can kill your body. Yeah, rather fear him who can kill your body and cast your soul into hell. Neither satan nor man can cast our souls anywhere. That's left to God! God said, the soul that sinneth, it shall surely die. But it is not the will of God Almighty that our souls sin.

This is why he sent Jesus to deliver us from our sins, not only to forgive us of our sins, but to deliver us, that our souls will not perish in hell. Hallelujah. But know this, God has not called any weak child of God.

The Bible says, let the weak say, I am strong. In Psalms 10, David is complaining because he feels that God is a far off in all these things that he is going through. And God seems not to be answering. And it seems like the wicked is getting the advantage over him. And he can't understand this, and he's looking. His eyes are on the wicked and how they are coming after his soul to destroy him.

How they even cross down and humble themselves to a point where they can deceive the servant of God, David. And David was able to perceive the wickedness and the evil plottings against him. But oh, David picked up courage because God began to manifest himself unto David.

And I let him know, you're not alone. The one with God is the majority. Though nations may rise against you, God, when God is on your side, he is more than all the nations because all the inhabitants of the earth are as grasshoppers in the eyes of God.

God is almighty. And it's good to know this God in whom we call upon. It's good to know that God cannot lie. It's good to know that his presence ever surrounds us. It's good to know that his angels are keeping charge over us. And if we have to die for his namesake, greater is our reward in heaven! Greater as a special reward for those who have been martyred for Jesus Christ!

So why do we fear? Men are dying every day, but for what cause? But if it's for Jesus' sake, bless the Lord. If we lay down our lives, the Lord said we shall take it up again. We are not destroyed. It's just a shortcut home, I always have said. Praise the name of Jesus.

Here's what the psalmist says in 118,

> *They compassed me about; yea, they compassed me about:*

> *But in the name of the LORD I will destroy them.*

Faith destroys many things. Faith says, I believe God.

And no weapon formed against me shall prosper.

The Lord helped me. Isn't it good to have the Lord on your side? Isn't it good to know that God Almighty is on your side? And no matter what man will try to do to make you fall, to make you stumble and fall, glory be to God, they can't get it done.

Because when God speaks a word, nothing can stop God. God will move heaven and earth for one person who believes him. Hallelujah. I've seen God do it! I've seen God move on behalf of his own. The enemy of our souls would say, aha, aha. So would we have it. But God says, aha, aha, down you go.

Who's given David this strength and this courage to stand up and say, in the name of the Lord, in the name of the Lord, I will destroy them. And we know the history of David. Glory be to God. He was a soldier, a mighty, valiant soldier. And all the men that were with him were just as valiant as David, warriors.

But see, our weapons are not carnal. Like David's weapons of old. David had one of the greatest weapons God ever gave the children of men; he had the weapon of prayer. This is why we have the book of Psalms. David, crying unto God and others who helped write the book of Psalms, wrote their prayers and their songs down.

They believed God. But David didn't stop just for praying. David would get up, pick up his sword, and fight. Hallelujah. He brought down not only Goliath, but he also brought down many strongholds of the devil. Because he was valiant to do so, he was anointed of God to do so in his day.

But Jesus tells us, thou shalt not kill. Hallelujah. He said, our weapons are not carnal. We don't take up the weapons that men on this earth are trained with. Our weapons are still the same: prayer, faith, righteousness, truth. We're determined to believe God. We're determined to call on the Lord. Our weapon is perseverance, watchfulness, glory be to God.

There is no weapon on earth that can destroy the weapons that God has given us. Most of all, the sword of the Spirit is the word of God. And that word is powerful. It's the living word and the written word. The living word abiding in us and praying us through. Hallelujah.

And the written word before us that we can boldly come into and open every day or any time of the day or night, and know that whatsoever the promises of God are, they are yea and amen to them that believe him. So we stand upon the greatest weapon of all. God's word is our deliverance.

The centurion said to Jesus Christ, you don't have to come into my home. Just speak the word, speak the word. He realized that Jesus was one of authority. And dear ones, we must realize it also that God's word never changes.

It's the same yesterday, today, and forever. The word of God. We stand upon the word of God, and the Lord will show himself excellent and mighty towards those who believe the word of God.

When you read the word, you pray it. You pray it back to God. Hallelujah. I made the mistake of listening to a preacher one time in my early days. He said, you don't have to remind God of what he says. He knows what he's already spoken.

And I stopped, and I stopped seeing God move. The one thing I have learned and I will never allow the enemy to rob me ever again. That's when you say 'Lord, you said…' and you start quoting God's word back before the throne of grace. God loves it. He hears it, and he says, there's one that believe what I have spoken. I'm willing to manifest my power. I'm willing to manifest my glory. I'm willing to fight their battles because they believe in God.

That's what God is looking for today. Will you dare believe God? The devil will tell you it's not for this day. But oh dear ones, it's more so today than ever because this is the end of the last days. Hallelujah.

We see the powers of darkness at work. We see the enemy in a frenzy to overthrow the church of Jesus Christ, which he can not do. But he's trying. He's trying, and he doesn't have wisdom or knowledge or the fear of God to give up and say I'm defeated because he's insane. And you can't stop an insane person until God overthrows, and God shall overthrow him. But in the meantime, he purposes to destroy nations and people because he's after the souls of men.

But it's up to us, the church of Jesus Christ, to rise up and put on Jesus and gird up the loins of our minds and say like David, in the name of the Lord, I will destroy the works of the devil. I will destroy him over all the nations. I will destroy his works that the glorious word of God may go forth and bring deliverance to the captives!

God's word is powerful. There's nothing on the face of this earth that can match the word of God when God's people believe him. There is no power, there is no authority that can match the word of God. It stands alone, and it's pure, and it's true, and it's righteous and holy.

And God is waiting, He's looking for somebody somewhere that believes in God that he might prove his word and work through mightily. Will you be that someone? Hallelujah. The psalmist says,

> *The LORD is my strength and song,*
>
> *And is become my salvation.*

*The voice of rejoicing and salvation is in the
tabernacles of the righteous:*

The right hand of the LORD doeth valiantly.

God is willing to work; He's willing to work valiantly.

The right hand of the LORD is exalted:

The right hand of the LORD doeth valiantly.

The Lord Jesus Christ,

I shall not die, but live,

And declare the works of the LORD.

The LORD hath chastened me sore:

But he hath not given me over unto death.

Open to me the gates of righteousness:

I will go into them, and I will praise the LORD:

You see, dear ones, it's through the power of praise. It's
through the thanksgiving and praise and prayer. It's time to
praise God. Whatever you're going through, don't hang
your head in sorrow. You rise up from there and lift up your
heads, Oh ye gates, and let the everlasting glory of God
come in and lift you up higher and higher and praise and
exalt his name continually in the name of Jesus Christ.

God be with you till we meet again. Amen and amen.

The Lord Our Confidence II

First Aired Feb 14th, 1999

Glory to God. We praise the Lord for his goodness and for his mercies that he has shown us. Forever, God is good and merciful to those who love him throughout all eternity.

It will be the mercies of God that endure forever upon us who love him. Everyone who passes over onto the other side can say it was God's mercies that brought me here, safe into the kingdom of God. We give God the glory, we give him the praise for the victory that he has given unto us and for blessing us to be on the air, to speak his word unto those that love him and unto those that he's after, that he's wooing unto himself and even to his enemies.

Praise God, we thank God for the word of God. We're still ministering under the subject, the Lord, our confidence. Surely God is our confidence. We have been looking and watching the different events that are happening in our nation and in the world abroad, and we're seeing all manner of sorrows and sicknesses and much travail coming upon the children of men, but God is our stay. God is our salvation, and I love to lift up his name. I love to share the word of God, to give men to know that God is good, no matter what we see, no matter the condition of man and the condition of man's hearts and the wars and the rumors of wars and the killing fields and so forth.

God is yet good and merciful and kind and long-suffering. The Lord is our confidence. The Lord is our shepherd, and he watches over us, and he longs for the world to come unto him.

The mercies of the Lord are longing for mankind to awake and see their need for God. God will not force Himself on any person. God is a holy God.

He's righteous, and he's true in all his works. God is merciful and good and true, and he is so willing to deliver man from sin, to deliver man from himself, to deliver man from the world and from the devil. And the word is going forth continually around the world for this very cause.

But at the same time, the word of God speaks, the living word speaks, whosoever will, let them come. Let them come and drink of the water of life freely. Whosoever will…

So that gives us to know that it's up to us. It's up to our will what we will allow to happen with our lives. But God is not held accountable if we do not give our lives over to him. He has already paid the price, and he is so willing and so loving and so patient. But time is running out for the children of men. And this is why the trumpet is being sounded in God's holy hill.

The trumpeters are blowing the trumpets. Praise the Lord, mightily used of God that the ear might hear and the soul might see and be converted. Hallelujah.

Let us pray. Precious Father, we come before the throne of grace in the name of Jesus. And we give you honor, and we give you glory. We give you the praise. We give thanks unto you because you are good and your mercies endure forever. We give you the praise because you're worthy to be praised.

We give you the honor because there's none to honor but you, Lord. When we look at all the facts, when our eyes are open, and we see only you, Lord, ought to be honored so highly and so greatly. No one but you, your love has given us this opportunity to even stand in your presence, to bow our heads before you, to call upon your name.

You've done it. You've made it possible. So we give you the honor, the glory, and the dominion; it's ever yours. Praise your holy name. Thank you for your goodness that you've shown unto us the children of men throughout all generations. Thank you for the confidence that you've put in our hearts that we can trust you.

We can walk with you in peace and harmony. We can love you. We can fellowship with you. Because you've given us Jesus, that open door to bring us before the throne of grace. Thank you for the heart that you have converted in us. Thank you for the soul that you have saved.

Praise God. Thank you for the word of God that you've written upon the table of our hearts and in our minds. We thank you. It is you, Lord, that have done this great work. It is you, Lord, who is keeping us and not we ourselves. But we have no knowledge, no understanding, to be able to keep ourselves.

It is you, Lord. We've given our lives unto you. And it's you who is keeping us from falling.

You're the one, amen, whom we depend upon. You are our confidence. You are our strength.

And I ask that your word will go forth this day under the unction of the Holy Spirit of God. That you will touch the lives that are listening. That you will strengthen each one, Lord God, that are calling upon your name.

That you will give clarity, power, and strength to those who desire you. And that desire to know the way of the Lord. Praise God that you would give them the shelter and the confidence in their innermost being.

That you will never leave them nor forsake them. Bless those, Lord God, amen, that are outside of the kingdom of God. Bless them to come and hear the word of God. And let the faith of God arise in their hearts. And help them to hear, help them to perceive and receive your engrafted word. That they might be converted and their souls be healed.

Hallelujah. Deal with our enemies, O God. Deal with them, O God, as none other can do but you. In the name of Jesus Christ. Those that the enemy would use to oppose us, to war against us. Bring down the strongholds of the devil. Cast them down to the pit. Cast them to hell where it belongs. In the name of Jesus, help them to gather up the loins of their minds and be sober.

It's vain to fight against the anointed of God. For you said, upon this rock I build my church. And the gates of hell shall not prevail against it.

Hallelujah. Break the yokes and fetters. Break the hand of the wickedness of the devil, Lord God. Break his bands asunder. Cut his cords asunder. In the name of Jesus.

And loose them from his evil clutches. Set them at liberty to call upon your name. And give them utterance before thee. You're merciful, God. You're forgiving. You're not willing that any man perish. Glory be to God. Those who will willfully oppose you, no matter how gracious you are. Give them their just dessert.

Give them what's coming. Give them what's due. But they have no fear of God and have sworn to war against you. Bring them down. Bring them down where they belong. In Jesus' name. Thy will be done, thy kingdom come. Send forth thy ministering angels and thy flames of fire. To minister for the needs of the saints, Lord.

Time is winding up, and we need you. We need your saving grace. We need your power, Lord God, to sustain us in these days. These closing hours. Bless your holy name. Let the victory of the Lord be wrought in each heart that will come after you. Praise the Lord of hosts. Psalms 40.

It is written, the benefits of having confidence in God and He prefers obedience over sacrifice. This is the psalm of David, the chief musician. He says,

I waited patiently for the Lord.

Patiently.

And he inclined unto me and heard my cry.

This is a key factor here. The word patiently. I waited patiently. The word of God tells us in the New Testament. In your patience possess ye your souls. Many times, we get excited. We want God to hurry. Hurry and do this. Hurry and do that. Glory hallelujah.

But God, in waiting for us, is working out a far greater work. That is needful to be wrought in us. But we are not to give up. Hallelujah. We are to wait on the Lord. In the word of God, as I ministered not long ago. The psalmist is saying, wait on the Lord and be of good courage. Wait, I say, on the Lord. God is sure. His word is sure. And your prayers are being heard.

They're put in a golden vial, and they're on the altar in heaven. And when God is ready to answer. He speaks to the angels to open the vials. Your prayers, your sweet-smelling odors coming up out of those golden vials unto God. And God sends the answer speedily in its time. So wait patiently on the Lord. He will not forsake us. He will not forsake you.

Don't be weary. Don't give up and say, oh, the Lord will not answer. Why won't he hear? Trust in the Lord. Have confidence in your God. He doeth all things well. And he's always on time. Don't run before him. Do not speak evil against him. Do not curse your God. Watch yourselves.

Watch and pray. Continue in prayer. Perseverance is one of God's great virtues. So persevere. Ask God for the strength to persevere and continue in prayer.

He said,

> *I waited patiently for the LORD;*
>
> *And he inclined unto me, and heard my cry.*
>
> *He brought me up also out of an horrible pit, out of the miry clay,*
>
> *And set my feet upon a rock, and established my goings.*
>
> *He established my goings.*

You see, there are appointed times for God to work. We don't know ourselves. And we don't know the path that we should take except to follow Jesus.

But there are many obstacles. There are many things that will rob us of the glory of God if it were not for the virtue of patience. As we patiently wait upon the Lord, God is working out a far greater thing in our innermost being.

And the stumbling blocks and the snares and the pitfalls that the enemy of our souls has laid privately or secretly against us to make us stumble and fall. We would go headlong into those snares and headlong into those pits if we did not know how to wait upon God. So learn this great virtue. Hallelujah.

God will establish His children. He will direct our path. He will guide us and lead us in a plain path because of our enemies. Hallelujah. Put your confidence in God.

He says,

> *And he hath put a new song in my mouth,*

A new song.

> Even praise unto our God:
>
> Many shall see it, and fear,
>
> And shall trust in the LORD.

They shall see the new work of grace, that new joy, that new gladness, that new song of praise because you dared to have confidence in God. And the Lord hath manifested Himself.

He has heard, and He has answered and delivered out of the pit and out of the snare of the fowler and set you upon a rock and established your goings. He made you, He caused you to be anchored in that rock. Made you steadfast and unmovable, and others will see this mighty work of grace, and they will honor the God that you serve. Hallelujah.

> *And he hath put a new song in my mouth, even*
>
> *praise unto our God:*
>
> *Many shall see it, and fear,*
>
> *And shall trust in the LORD.*

Isn't it marvelous to know that as one or many watch your life, that because of the way you live, they will choose to follow the living God. Well, that's what Jesus means by ye are lights… ye are lights set upon a hill. You're glorifying God with your life, and the light that is in us comes from God. God illuminates us. God shines in us.

He does this mighty work of grace in us, and that's continual. And as He works His mighty work and manifests His glorious grace, others can't help but see it, and they can't help but glorify the God that you serve. And many will desire Him just as you know Him.

> *Blessed is that man that maketh the LORD his trust,*

You want to be blessed? You don't have to go and pay anything to any sorcerer or any soothsayer or wizard or witch. Just get blessed of God. God's blessing comes upon those who trust Him and fear Him. You don't have to go through anyone but Jesus. No one but Jesus because He's that door to the Father. Glory, hallelujah.

You don't need any gadgets or gimmicks. All you need is faith in God to believe the Word of God. That's your blessing. Praise God.

> *Blessed is that man that maketh the LORD his trust,*
>
> *And respecteth not the proud, nor such as turn aside to lies.*

The proud you don't respect. Many are turning aside to lies, and they'll bombard you because you are of the truth. They'll despise and hate you. They'll put snares in your path because you abide in Jesus, who is the truth. Glory, hallelujah.

But these are the blessings of the Lord upon you. To be able to know the difference between a lie and the truth is a blessing. Many minds are mesmerized, bewitched because they cannot differentiate between what's right and what's wrong, between a lie and the truth.

And the Bible says many shall follow their pernicious ways and be damned. So it's a blessing to know the truth, to be able to be enlightened by God. Buy the truth and sell it not.

You buy the truth and sell it not. Self in every one of us hates God, according to Galatians 5. Self in every one of us, sinner or saint, hates God. Self cannot please God. And this is why Jesus said, deny yourself. Pick up your cross and follow me. Your responsibility is to God.

This is why we're here on the face of this earth. To live unto God before the children of men. Bless the Lord. Hallelujah. Blessed is that man who maketh the Lord his trust. Verse 5,

> Many, O LORD my God,
>
> *Are* thy wonderful works *which* thou hast done,
>
> And thy thoughts *which are* to us-ward:

You see, God thinks of us constantly. God is thinking about us. And everything that God has promised us is because he loves us. When we were not reconciled to God because of the sin of Eve and Adam, God in due time sent his only begotten son to ransom us because he was always thinking on the fellowship, the sweet communion that he had with Adam and Eve in the garden of Eden.

And God wanted it back. Here and there, God would have someone righteous on the face of the earth. But God wanted a people of all nations that he might fellowship with by his Spirit. And bless his holy name. God has won.

God has people of all nations under the sun, all colors, all sizes, all tongues. God has a people out of these nations. And according to the book of Revelation, these people whom God is fellowshipping with right now by his spirit shall bring their glory out of these nations into the kingdom of heaven when Jesus comes.

So God is always thinking about us. His thoughts are towards us. Bless his holy name.

> *They cannot be reckoned up in order unto thee:*
>
> *If I would declare and speak of them,*
>
> *They are more than can be numbered.*

The thoughts of God concerning us, the children of men. This is why the Psalmist asks, what is man that thou art mindful of him? You know what it is? It's the soul that's in that clay body. That soul comes from God. The breath that we breathe… It's on loan to us from God, whether we are saved or not. That breath that we inhale and exhale belongs to God. Hallelujah. It belongs to God. And that's why he's mindful of us.

Anything that his presence is abiding in, he's mindful of. And his thoughts are numerous towards us. This is why God gave his only begotten Son that we might be. That we might be reconciled back to him and brought in harmony and sweet fellowship and sweet communion with him. The Psalmist said,

If I would declare and speak of them,

They are more than can be numbered.

So we can never, never, never give up on his thoughts towards us, if we are alert and awake to the love of God. But God doesn't want us to always be recipients of his love and never give love. And many are guilty of such a thing.

Bless me, bless me. But when God gives, he wants us in turn to give back. Give to others. As we give, God is blessing us the more. Press down, shaking together and running over. The Lord said, men would give into our bosom. Why? Because we are giving. We are giving his love. We are sharing his love. And sharing the blessings of the Lord with one another. Bless his holy name. In verse six,

Sacrifice and offering thou didst not desire;

See this? It's not in what we can give materially. He said,

Mine ears hast thou opened:

Burnt offering and sin offering hast thou not required.

It's already done; Jesus gave himself the sacrifice for the children of men.

Then said I, Lo, I come:

In the volume of the book it is written of me,

That's what Jesus said. And the psalmist is prophesying of what Jesus is saying to the father.

Sacrifice and offering thou didst not desire;

But Jesus said,

Lo, I come:

In the volume of the book it is written of me, 8I delight to do thy will, O my God:

Yea, thy law is within my heart.

My heart…And that's where God is knocking. At the heart. Just as the Son of God, the only begotten Son of God, delighted to do his will. God is knocking on the door of our hearts that we might open unto him and delight to do his will. It is time to be faithful and true to the living God. God be with you until we meet again.

Raised Up Together

First Aired Sept 9th, 2001

In the name of Jesus, we come before you, thanking God for Jesus Christ and who he is in our lives. Surely he is the Savior, the King of kings and Lord of lords, as we know him to be, we that are redeemed, and we give him the glory and the honor and the praise that's due unto his name, before all of you that are listening. We thank God for you who have tuned in to God's Holy Mountain broadcast, and we trust that this ministry has been a tool, a blessing to build up the Christians and to call those who are weak back to the faith of Jesus Christ, to your rightful place in his kingdom.

And to you that have never known Christ as your personal Savior, we give you the opportunity, amen, and the invitation to come as you hear the word of God preached, hear the word of God taught, and surrender your lives unto him.

We get such beautiful letters, especially from abroad, telling us how many have gathered themselves together in the community in which they live, some of their church members. We come on at different hours in different countries abroad, but what they write is just about the same, no matter where their letters are coming from.

Telling us how they are gathered together around the radio to listen to God's Holy Mountain broadcast and how the Lord is strengthening their lives, and even challenging them to a higher walk in Christ Jesus. And many are being saved just listening to what God is calling his own that are already redeemed, that are washed in the blood, unto… Praise God in the highest.

And from the book of Ephesians, what a beautiful and glorious book of revelation of Christ and his body, the church of Jesus Christ, that God has given the writer of this book, Ephesians, to the apostle Paul, amen. I'll be skipping from certain verses in the book, not just one particular chapter, but before we start into the word, let us pray.

Because we need to know and to receive from God, the Father, the power and the ability to hear and to understand and receive his word.

Precious Father, before the throne of grace, we come boldly in Jesus' name, the name that you've given us to approach your throne. We boldly come. Praise God, asking Father for thy strength, thy power, thy wisdom, thy knowledge, and understanding. Reveal your mysteries unto us, even as you did to the apostle Paul. As we go into the book of Ephesians, enlighten our eyes that we might behold the glory of the Lord Jesus Christ and the glory that you have with your body, the church of Jesus Christ worldwide.

Thy will be done, thy kingdom come with greater authority, greater anointing, greater power, Lord, as we understand and you release the power of God within us, that we might walk upright before you and be all together pleasing in your sight and bind the forces of hell, Lord God, that would come to rob the people, we pray in Jesus' name. We bind on earth that which is contrary to your will, and we bring it down. We cast it down under your feet in the authoritative name of Jesus Christ. Amen and amen.

In the first chapter of the book of Ephesians, the word of God tells us in verse three,

> *Blessed be the God and Father of our Lord Jesus Christ, who hath blessed us with all spiritual blessings in heavenly places in Christ:*

God, the Father, has blessed us, the church of Jesus Christ, the body of Christ. We who are washed and made clean by the blood of Jesus, He has blessed us, this is amazing, with all spiritual blessings in heavenly places in Christ. This is where we are to live. We know that physically we are in this world, glory to God, we are bound in a physical body, but we who are born again, we ascend unto the kingdom of heaven, in heaven, in heavenly places by faith, by the glorious gift of faith.

Whatever is revealed unto us concerning God, the Father and God, the Son, God, the Holy Spirit, and the church, the body of Christ, is revealed unto us by the faith of God. Amen. And verse four says,

> *according as he hath chosen us in him before the foundation of the world, that we should be holy and without blame before him in love:*

In the love of God, not the natural love that so many of us have known and have been partakers of, because natural love is not the real love of God. Natural love picks and chooses whom they desire to love. But in the eyes of God, when we are born again, we love because God is love, and we love through the love of God to all humanity.

We embrace humanity as God has made humanity because of his love, his glorious love. And Jesus said as he was given out the mind of his father. He told us that the world would know that we are his disciples if we love one another, not picking and choosing whom we desire to love, but we love through the eyes of God.

We love pitifully. We love forgivingly. We love because it's the handiwork of God. Mankind, the soul of man, is the handiwork of God. And we love because we have been brought into a higher realm of the love of God, a God pay love, God's love, because God is love.

And when we are redeemed, the love of God takes over our hearts. And this is what the apostle Paul means. The things that we once hated, we now love because we are transformed into the image of Jesus Christ. We have taken on God in us. Amen. And he just moves right on in. And he loves through us. Bless his holy name. And he says,

> *having predestinated us unto the adoption of children by Jesus Christ to himself, according to the good pleasure of his will, to the praise of the glory of his grace, wherein he hath made us accepted in the beloved.*

God makes us accepted. He chooses us and accepts us because of Jesus Christ, who has redeemed us. Isn't that marvelous? We're redeemed by the love of God through Jesus Christ. Whoever Jesus washes with his blood, that person is automatically accepted by God.

And the same love that God has for his only begotten son, he loves us with that same passion, that same love, nothing less, because he sees the blood of his son covering us. The blood of Jesus Christ, the image of his dear son has taken its abode within us. And just as Christ was accepted.

Look over in verse 19,

> *and what is the exceeding greatness of his power to us-ward who believe, according to the working of his mighty power, which he wrought in Christ, when he raised him from the dead, and set him at his own right hand in the heavenly places, far above all principality, and power, and might, and dominion, and every name that is named, not only in this world, but also in that which is to come: and hath put all things under his feet, and gave him to be the head over all things to the church, which is his body, the fulness of him that filleth all in all.*

That's why God loves us because of the union of the body of Christ with his Son. We're called into oneness. It's what Jesus prayed before the Father in the 17th chapter of John.

Father, I pray that they be one, even as we are one. So, Jesus Christ, when he hung on that cross, he was uniting us predestinated already. Those who are going to believe on him and accept him for who he is.

Jesus Christ was uniting us with God our maker, through himself, through Jesus. He had to give his life a ransom for us to be redeemed.

That our sins might be forgiven, that our names might be in heaven already on record, predestinated because God knows the end from the beginning. It's not that the Lord has picked and chosen who's to be saved, but knowing who we are, knowing the end of this world, knowing eternity, because God is eternal, already knowing the works of men before the works were performed.

He already knew the heart of man who would accept his gift of love, his gift of redemption, who would come under the blood covenant with his son, whom he has sent, his only begotten son, Jesus.

He already knew, and therefore, we who have been redeemed have already been predestinated by God because he knows the end from the beginning. But we make the choice. We are here making choices, good or evil; we are here to make choices.

And we who make Jesus Christ our choice. God has already chosen us. It's his will. He's calling many unto righteousness, many unto holiness, the holiness of God. And understand, I am not talking about any denomination. I am talking about God, the person who is holy, who is righteous altogether.

God has already ordained that we come into this beautiful, high, and lofty walk of holiness, of righteousness. Jesus Christ in verse 17,

> *that the God of our Lord Jesus Christ, the Father of glory, may give unto you the spirit of wisdom and revelation in the knowledge of him:*

That's the will of God through Jesus Christ. That God… the God of our Lord Jesus Christ, may give unto you the spirit of wisdom. This is what we have need of church believers and you who are listening. We need the wisdom of God. We need the spirit of wisdom. We need to know and understand Christ to be revealed unto us.

Wisdom and revelation in the knowledge of him who he is. God has called us to sit with him in heavenly places with Jesus Christ. We have been made joint heirs. Joint heirs into the kingdom of God Almighty through Jesus Christ.

What a high and lofty call. How many are taking heed to that call? How many are actually coming into that place of highness, of royalty, with Jesus Christ? Jesus didn't come down here as a poor pauper.

Jesus Christ came from heaven. With all the riches and all the glory and all the honor that he had with the Father. And he came down to share the kingdom of heaven with us to redeem those that would listen, those who would hear the word of God preached. Those that would believe and those who would accept the word of the Lord Jesus.

That's why he is called the living Word. He came as the living Word, telling us what the Father has already wrought for us, praise God in the highest, what his purpose and his plan is… The redemption for all humanity. For all humanity, it's not for a few.

It's for everyone that believe. But we must believe the report given of Jesus Christ. Because he is the one God the Father sent to shed his blood for the remission of our sins.

That we might be cleansed from all our sins and all ungodliness. Let me show you what ungodliness is, why God tells us to be holy. Over in Romans, the first chapter. The Lord is talking through the apostle, amen, the apostle Paul. Verse 13,

> *Now I would not have you ignorant, brethren, that oftentimes I purposed to come unto you, (but was let hitherto,) that I might have some fruit among you also, even as among other Gentiles. I am debtor both to the Greeks, and to the Barbarians; both to the wise, and to the unwise.*

What a man of God.

> *So, as much as in me is, I am ready to preach the gospel to you that are at Rome also. For I am not ashamed of the gospel of Christ: for it is the power of God unto salvation to every one that believeth;*

Everyone that believe it. It is the power of God unto salvation. It takes the power of God to bring us unto salvation. A sinner just can't merely come and say okay. We are drawn unto God by his spirit. The power of God.

We are listening to his word. In order to be able to understand the love of God reaching out to us. It takes the power of God to enlighten our ears and minds to what God is saying and what his purpose is.

It's the will of God to save that which is lost. Jesus Christ came to save that which is lost. And he is yet in the saving business because God loves humanity. God loves the souls of men. And Paul says he is not ashamed of the gospel of Christ, for it is the power of God unto salvation for everyone that believeth.

> *it is the power of God unto salvation to every one that believeth; to the Jew first, and also to the Greek. For therein is the righteousness of God revealed from faith to faith:*

It takes the faith of God in order to understand his righteousness. And he will reveal it. There's no other way. It must be revealed unto us. And we as humanity must see our need for redemption. We must see it in order to ask and receive his great salvation.

> *as it is written, The just shall live by faith. For the wrath of God is revealed from heaven against all ungodliness and unrighteousness of men, who hold the truth in unrighteousness;*

Many know the truth. Many know it. But still bound by sin, by unrighteousness, not being transformed. Not being renewed in the mind, not allowing the Holy Spirit to transform their heart.

Many know the truth.

No one is going to hold God accountable in that last day.
Because God is willing to reveal the truth.

They had an experience of God.

Those that had once been enlightened became vain in their
minds and their imaginations. Instead of pulling down the
wicked imaginations. They lifted up the wicked
imaginations of the mind, and became that much more
foolish. And the word of God says,

Listen! This is the wrath of God. When God gives you up to uncleanness. When you have come into the knowledge of God, and have been quickened by his Spirit, and you go contrary to his will…

The word of God says the wrath of God comes upon the children of disobedience. When you've once been enlightened to his truth. But did not embrace his truth, did not love his truth. Holding His truth in unrighteousness. Allowing yourself to continue in wickedness and abomination. Here's what God has allowed to happen.

> *Wherefore God also gave them up.*

Why? Because they chose to take themselves out of the love of God, out from his holiness, out from his righteousness, out from abiding in his truth! And being a doer of the word.

> *God also gave them up to uncleanness through the lusts of their own hearts, to dishonour their own bodies between themselves: who changed the truth of God into a lie,*

And so many are doing it today.

> *and worshipped and served the creature more than the Creator, who is blessed for ever.*

God said thou shalt not have any other god before me. And man is allowing anything else. Serving and worshiping the creature more than the creator.

> *For this cause God gave them up unto vile affections*

In other words, God has turned you over to unclean spirits, demon spirits. Oh, I know you don't hear this kind of talk. But it's the word of God. I am reading out from the Word of God!

> *For this cause God gave them up unto vile affections: for even their women did change the natural use into that which is against nature: and likewise also the men, leaving the natural use of the woman, burned in their lust one toward another; men with men working that which is unseemly, and receiving in themselves that recompence of their error which was meet. And even as they did not like*

See, there's the will of man again…

> *even as they did not like to retain God in their knowledge,*

God the holy, God the righteous, God the truth.

> *God gave them over to a reprobate mind,*

that's going in a perverse way.

> *to do those things which are not convenient; being filled with all unrighteousness,*

He names it.

> *fornication, wickedness, covetousness, maliciousness; full of envy, murder, debate, deceit, malignity; whisperers, backbiters,*

People would not think that whisperers would be this way in the eyes of God. This is unclean… This is unclean because God gives us boldness to speak one to another. In love. See, that's the way of the Lord.

And any other way is contrary to what God has already ordained. And that's why we hear the words,

> *whisperers, backbiters, haters of God, despiteful, proud, boasters, inventors of evil things, disobedient to parents, without understanding*

And that's what God tells us to do in Proverbs. In all thy getting, get understanding, get the mind of Christ, and understand what's on his mind.

> *without understanding, covenantbreakers, without natural affection, implacable, unmerciful:*

Showing no mercy, self always first, or die.

> *who knowing the judgment of God, that they which commit such things are worthy of death,*

Eternal damnation from the presence of God.

> *not only do the same, but have pleasure in them that do them.*

In other words, those who do the same thing that's in their hearts. They take pleasure in such a people or such a kind of person as that. But Christ Jesus has brought the church into a high and lofty place above all of these things.

We're redeemed from all of these wicked things. We're washed. Our sins are never held against us when we continue on to follow after Jesus.

Jesus Christ, verse 21 of Ephesians 1,

> *far above all principality*

That's where Christ dwells. He's set on the right hand of the Father in heavenly places.

> *far above all principality, and power, and might,*

Power of darkness… Jesus Christ is far above it because he is light.

> *and dominion, and every name that is named, not only in this world, but also in that which is to come: and hath put all things under his feet,*

And that's where we are, we sit with Christ, expecting and performing. Carrying out the things that God is expecting of us, to perform until it comes for us. Amen. That's where we are with Christ.

And if we choose to take ourselves out from such a high and lofty place. We bring ourselves under the wrath of God. And who can abide under His wrath when that wrath is made manifest? God is calling us not unto the wrath of God.

But unto wholeness, wellness, blessings, and honor. And this choice is ours, dear ones. It's up to us. God be with you. And pray about these things as you seek his face. In Jesus name we pray. Amen.

In the House I

First Aired March 4th, 2001

In the 12th chapter of the Book of Romans, the Word of
God says,

> *I beseech you therefore, brethren, by the mercies of
> God,*

by the mercies of God,

> *that ye present your bodies a living sacrifice,*

You present your body. That's up to the will of the
individual or individuals to present their bodies, a living
sacrifice… holy. We are to present holy bodies, acceptable
unto God. See, God will not have anything thrown at Him,
not just anything, because He's a holy God. And God tells
us that we are to be holy even as He is holy.

So, when we give ourselves as sacrificial beings to Him, He
wants us holy, that He might accept us in His will. He said,

> *holy, acceptable unto God, which is your
> reasonable service. And be not conformed to this
> world: but be ye transformed by the renewing of
> your mind,*

Let your mind be renewed by the Spirit of God,

> *that ye may prove what is that good, and
> acceptable, and perfect, will of God.*

This is how we are to live in this world. Unto Him, we belong to Him when we are born into His kingdom by the Spirit of God and washed in the blood of the Son of God, Jesus Christ. Our names are written in the Lamb's Book of Life.

And then we have obligations, we have duties to perform in the eyes of God, and He has not left us to do it alone. Everything that we do, we live in the Spirit of God. We live by the Spirit of God. We live in the name of the Lord Jesus Christ. Whatever we do, whatever we think, it should be concerning the will of God through the power of God in Jesus Christ. Amen.

Jesus is the author and the finisher of our faith. So, it takes faith to present ourselves unto God. It takes faith to present ourselves wholly unto God. It takes faith to be found in the acceptable will of God and to be found in it perfectly. We are to prove what the perfect will of God is, not only the acceptable will, but the perfect will of God. And that's where our joy and our peace are, when we know that we are in His perfect will.

And I know that this may sound foreign, like a foreign language to many Christians, because many are not taught this. Many Christians are not taught this, but it's the truth, and it should not be overlooked. Because the Lord, when He comes back, He's coming back for a church that is full of holiness, full of righteousness, full of truth.

Amen. In other words, sinless. So, we live by the power of God. We live by the power of God that is in us. Now, over in the eighth chapter of Numbers in the Old Testament, here's how the Levites were made clean. I won't read it all, but in your spare time, in your leisure time, for greater understanding, it would be good to read the whole chapter.

Beginning at the 19th verse,

> *And I have given the Levites as a gift*

This is God speaking to Moses, the prophet of God.

> *And I have given the Levites as a gift to Aaron*

Aaron was the high priest,

> *and to his sons from among the children of Israel, to do the service of the children of Israel in the tabernacle of the congregation, and to make an atonement for the children of Israel: that there be no plague among the children of Israel, when the children of Israel come nigh unto the sanctuary.*

> *And Moses, and Aaron, and all the congregation of the children of Israel, did to the Levites according unto all that the LORD commanded Moses concerning the Levites, so did the children of Israel unto them.*

> *And the Levites were purified, and they washed their clothes; and Aaron offered them as an offering before the LORD; and Aaron made an atonement for them to cleanse them. And after that went the Levites in to do their service in the tabernacle of the congregation before Aaron, and before his sons: as the LORD had commanded Moses concerning the Levites, so did they unto them.*

You see, there's a process of cleansing. Amen. Our pastor told us many years ago,

"God took you out of the world… but now, He is taking the world out of you."

 See, it's twofold. God calls us from the world, from the world of sin, we call it Egypt. God calls his people out of Egypt from all pagan worship and so forth. See, when we are sinners, we are worshiping everything but God. Amen.

Yes, right here in the United States, anything that we put above God is idol worship. And that's where we're coming from, we're coming from a world of sin that is full of idolatry and full of wickedness. And the Lord brings us unto himself. And we come as a green olive tree. We come washed in the blood. Jesus washes our sins away.

But our spirits are still raw and unlearned. Our minds are not consumed with the Word of God. We're just coming to know that we were sinners and that God is God, our Father, and he has given us freely his son to cleanse us from our sins, that he might be our savior. And if we go any farther, we may know that our names are written in the Lamb's Book of Life. You might say, well, that's enough…

Well, that's enough if you're going to pass completely out of this world at that point. But if we are going to remain here in this world and remain children of God, remain free in spirit, remain free from that world that God has called us from, we're going to need to know that our spirits need cleansing. From all the things that we were accustomed to.

Some of us have come to the Lord at early ages, and some
at very old ages, some as little children. Little children
don't know that much about sinning, little ones.

But as you grow older, sin becomes greater and greater in
the heart and in the mind, in the lives of people. So, as we
come to the Lord, there are many things that we must
forsake to follow the Lord Jesus Christ. Now, the initial
work of salvation is done. The gift of God is eternal life.
And Jesus said we are his disciples if we obey what he said,
if we continue in obedience.

And some of us have come from stubbornness, from
rebellion, from doing our own thing, not subject to anyone,
declaring that we will never be subject to anyone. And so
we must learn that we've got to give that desire up when we
come to follow Jesus. We're not doing our own thing
anymore. We do not belong to ourselves. We do not do our
own will. We do not continue in our own way.

But we must forsake these things and allow the Holy Spirit
to make everything new within our minds and in our spirits
and in our hearts, that we might walk according to the will
of God that's written here in the Bible.

This book is our guide, and the Holy Spirit is given, the
Spirit of God is given to guide us through and give us
understanding of the meaning of what is written here in this
guide (the Bible) for our lives. So the more we learn of
Christ, the more we die to ourselves.

The Apostle Paul learned this. He said, I die daily. The more we draw near to Christ, the more we see that we must forsake and put off the old man, that we all together might be a complete new lump in Christ. Praise the Lord.

So here is a picture of what the children of God are to be like. As the Levites were, every one of us should be Levites in the eyes of God. Because when we come into the congregation of righteousness… remember what the Word of God says in Psalms, that the wicked shall not stand in the congregation of the righteous. Amen. Because when the righteousness of God is going forth in the congregation, wickedness will not be able to stand up in the presence of God.

You've got to make a decision. You cannot continue in wickedness because God is going to bring conviction by his spirit, and he's going to destroy it. If you will that you destroy it. You see, we cannot remain children of God and be rebellious against the instructions of holiness, the instructions of righteousness, the instructions of truth and peace and justice and love and equity. Because all of these things are of God. Amen!

So we have to do like the Levites, everything that the Holy Spirit will show us as we're seeking in the face of God. Lord wash me, Lord cleanse me, Lord purify me. Amen.

That's not just an initial work. It's every day of our lives. The more we learn of him, the more we are cleansed, the more we are purified. Because in the Word, Jesus told his disciples, now you're clean through the Word that I have spoken unto you. Not just my blood that has washed you initially, but my Word, as you obey my Word, as you receive my Word, as I give you my Word, you are cleansed if you receive my Word. Now you're clean!

And every day, there are decisions that we have to make. Lord, am I going to follow you wholeheartedly today? Or am I going to be partial in my love for you today? So that's a decision that we have to make daily. And I say daily because the Lord said, pick up your cross daily and follow me.

You see, this is how we present our bodies unto the Lord. Our bodies for service, but our bodies must be holy. This is in the house of the Lord. We are brought into the holy sanctuary of God on high, the kingdom of God I'm speaking of. And we are his tabernacles. We are his earthly tabernacles.

And he seeks to abide in us fully, not just in our minds, but in our spirits, in our hearts, in our bodies, in our souls. God wants every part of our being, and He will show us, he will instruct us in the way of righteousness, how to be well-pleasing in his sight. And this is what God is calling the church of Jesus Christ unto, because there has been a great falling away from this great walk of faith and love.

We speak of faith, but how much is our love for God? Are we willing to forsake all to follow him? As he left heaven, he left all, all of that beauty and splendor of being in the presence of his father to come to a world that was dark and cold and full of hatred and thorns and briars and death itself.

Are we willing to follow Jesus like he followed the Father in bringing his word to us? In Numbers, the 10th chapter, amen. Have your mighty way, Lord Jesus.

Numbers 10, verse 33,

> *And they departed from the mount of the LORD three days' journey: and the ark of the covenant of the LORD went before them in the three days' journey, to search out a resting place for them. And the cloud of the LORD was upon them by day, when they went out of the camp.*
>
> *And it came to pass, when the ark set forward, that Moses said, Rise up, LORD, and let thine enemies be scattered; and let them that hate thee flee before thee.*

Let them that hate thee flee before thee… and this is what God is saying today.

The ark of the Lord is Jesus Christ for us today. He's that ark of safety, and he's that ark that carries the word of life. Jesus says, the word that I speak unto you, they are spirit, and they are life, amen. And he said, I didn't come to speak my own words. You see, the ark of God is Jesus Christ for us today.

And our only safety, our only life, is in the ark, who is Jesus. Praise his holy name. And he says, here's what Moses said. And there are Moseses around today. And it came to pass when the ark set forward that Moses said, rise up, Lord, and let thine enemies be scattered. Let those who hate the instructions of righteousness be scattered.

Let those who hate the safety of God be scattered. There's no other way. There is no other way!

Either we are gathered unto Christ, or we are scattered. See, we're not our own. Jesus Christ, is that ark.

And he's compelling men and women, boys and girls every day to come into the ark of safety and be saved. But he's not going to receive us any old way. People say he loves you just as you are. Yes, he does. But he's not going to receive us just any old way. Amen.

He will receive us as we come unto him. But when we come to him, and he begins to teach us the way of righteousness, the way of the Lord, we are to do the way of righteousness. We are to perform it.

We want to put it all on Jesus Christ. Jesus Christ, the righteousness of God. Yes, but are we following that righteousness, or are we doing our own thing and saying, Lord, you bless it. You bless it. No, it doesn't work that way.

God will not alter his word. Praise the Lord of hosts. Look at Jesus back in the garden of Gethsemane. And he felt that cup of death coming upon him. And he's crying out to God with great sweat. Amen. As blood is dripping out of his veins and dripping out of his pores. And he's saying, Father, if it be thy will, let this cup pass from me. Meaning the cup of death.

And the father would not answer because it was already written that Jesus Christ would be the one to suffer for our sins, to bear our chastisement upon himself, and to bear our griefs and be stricken and smitten and rejected of men. And he's at this point, he's smitten, and he's rejected of men. And in just a few moments, they will be coming after him.

The high priest, the Jewish high priest, had sent soldiers already at that point to go and catch Jesus Christ, that he might be crucified. And Jesus is feeling this. And you think the father would answer his son? If it be thy will, let this cup be passed from me…No!

The word of God says in Isaiah 53, it pleased the Father. It pleased God that his son might be afflicted. Why? Because of His great love for humanity. God Almighty, His great love for humanity. He sent his Son to bear the reproach of death, to bear our sins, our infirmities, our diseases. Hallelujah.

So God, the father, in being solid was saying, no, my son, this cup will not pass from you. I have ordained that you taste death for everyone, for everyone, and then God said in Isaiah 53, My righteous servant shall justify many. Jesus Christ was a servant of God on that cross…dying! Hallelujah. Amen.

 And that righteous servant bore our sins. And this is why we are saved today. And shall we continue in sin that graced me abound? Nay! No, no, no, no, no.

Hallelujah. But we are to present our bodies, a living sacrifice. It's in the house. Holiness is in the house. Righteousness is in the house. Walking in truth is in the house. Hallelujah. In the house of clay!

And we bring in the house of clay, we bring these, these tabernacles, these, these earthly vessels into the place where we have set aside that we call church. And we come together as holy believers, righteous believers, lovers of God, lovers of the way of the Lord. And when we unite, there is power. There's greater love poured into our being. There's a greater understanding poured into our being.

And we're brought closer unto God. We're brought higher unto God. We're made deeper in God. Praise the Lord of hosts. And this is what God is calling his church back unto, as the first church had, amen, two thousand years ago, God is calling the church back. He's calling Zion back to a rightful place in Zion to be presented unto God continually, every day, holy and acceptable and well-pleasing in the eyes of the most high God.

And we can say, like Moses, rise up, Lord, and let thine enemies be scattered. Praise God and let them that hate thee flee from before thee. And to God be the glory in your life. Amen and amen.

In the House II

First Aired March 18th, 2001

Praise God, we give praise and honor to the Most High God, and we thank the Lord for the ability and the opportunity to come your way again in Jesus' name. And we thank the Lord for your tuning in to God's Holy Mountain broadcast.

I know by the grace of God that this ministry has been a blessing to those who want to grow up in the Lord. That's why we are here, and that's why this ministry is called, this radio broadcast is called, God's Holy Mountain. Amen. It's for those who desire to be brought up higher in the Lord and to partake of His divine ways every day. Jesus is coming. Amen.

In the fifth chapter of Galatians, you that have your Bibles, please turn with us there. And also in the 13th chapter of Saint Matthew.

Let us pray, God, my Father, our rock and our salvation, in the name of Thy Son Jesus, we come before the throne of grace boldly. And we're asking that you would have preeminence over your word this day, that you would give this vessel of clay, utterance by the Holy Spirit, in the precious, powerful name of Jesus Christ.

Thy will be done. Take the audience's minds and hearts into your captivity right now. And let Thy word go forth unhindered. And let Thy seed fall on good ground this day, in Jesus' mighty name. Hallelujah.

Let all the opposing forces of hell be bound. And the principalities and the powers of the air, we bring down, we command to be brought down, we pull down in the authority of Jesus' name. And we surrender everything under the feet of the Lord Jesus Christ. Amen and amen. Thy word, Lord, is power. Bring forth the power of Thy word this day.

In the fifth chapter of Galatians, the Word of God says,

> *Stand fast therefore in the liberty wherewith Christ hath made us free, and be not entangled again with the yoke of bondage.*

And over in the 13th chapter of Matthew, the Lord is talking about the sower that went forth to sow the seed. It's the seed of God, the planting of the Lord, the planting of the Lord Jesus Christ. That great and mighty sower, mighty apostle from on high, the mighty evangelist from on high.

> *The same day went Jesus out of the house, and sat by the sea side. And great multitudes were gathered together unto him, so that he went into a ship, and sat; and the whole multitude stood on the shore.*
>
> *And he spake many things unto them in parables, saying, Behold, a sower went forth to sow; and when he sowed, some seeds fell by the way side, and the fowls came and devoured them up: some fell upon stony places, where they had not much earth:*

*and when the sun was up, they were scorched; and
because they had no root, they withered away. And
some fell among thorns; and the thorns sprung up,
and choked them: but other fell into good ground,
and brought forth fruit, some an hundredfold, some
sixtyfold, some thirtyfold. Who hath ears to hear, let
him hear.*

Whoever will open their ears to hear, thus saith the Lord
here, let him hear. The disciples wanted to know, what do
you mean by this? And Jesus answered, verse 11,

*He answered and said unto them, Because it is
given unto you to know the mysteries of the kingdom
of heaven, but to them it is not given.*

Why? Is he showing partiality? No... Jesus knew those who
belonged to God. He had discernment of spirit. He
perceived those who were contrary to what the Word was
saying. And that's why he said, He that has ears to
hear…Who has ears to hear, let him hear.

But he said to his disciples in verse 12,

*For whosoever hath, to him shall be given, and he
shall have more abundance: but whosoever hath
not, from him shall be taken away even that he
hath. Therefore speak I to them in parables:
because they seeing see not;*

They are looking, but they are not perceiving.

> *and hearing they hear not, neither do they understand.*

They are hearing… but they are not hearing according to the Holy Spirit.

> *neither do they understand. And in them is fulfilled the prophecy of Esaias, which saith,*
>
> *By hearing ye shall hear, and shall not understand;*
>
> *And seeing ye shall see, and shall not perceive:*
>
> *For this people's heart is waxed gross,*
>
> *And their ears are dull of hearing,*
>
> *And their eyes they have closed;*

God didn't close them, and the devil didn't close them. They, because of the condition of their hearts… they closed their eyes.

> *Lest at any time they should see with their eyes,*
>
> *And hear with their ears,*
>
> *And should understand with their heart,*

See, at any time, any time the heart is open, any time the ear is open, any time… lest at any time, that's what Jesus said. Did you see it? Verse 15,

> *Lest at any time they should see with their eyes,*
>
> *And hear with their ears,*

And should understand with their heart,

And should be converted,

That means changed

and I should heal them.

Healing belongs to the children of God. Not only from physical disabilities and afflictions, but to the soul, and the spirit, and the heart, and the mind, the Lord will heal and bring enlightenment.

And he said to his disciples,

But blessed are your eyes, for they see: and your ears, for they hear.

In other words, you're hearing when I speak, then you understand what I'm saying.

For verily I say unto you, That many prophets and righteous men have desired to see those things which ye see,

See what I'm saying? I said to you earlier, church, how in the Old Testament, everything, every book of the Bible was written. There was something they had to say about the Lamb of God, Jesus Christ, the true Savior of the world, the only Savior of all mankind. He said,

For verily I say unto you, That many prophets and righteous men have desired to see those things which ye see, and have not seen them; and to hear those things which ye hear, and have not

heard them. Hear ye therefore the parable of the sower.

Then he breaks it down to them most clearly.

When anyone heareth the word of the kingdom,

Anyone…

and understandeth it not, then cometh the wicked one,

Meaning satan,

and catcheth away that which was sown in his heart.

It was already put in the heart, do you hear this? Catcheth away that which was sown in his heart.

This is he which received seed by the way side.

Now it's up to us to take this word and judge ourselves, amen, with the word.

But he that received the seed into stony places, the same is he that heareth the word, and anon with joy receiveth it;

Remember how the word would go forth and people would be on their feet, and they're rejoicing and so forth, and you ask them later, what was it all about? Well, honey… this is what I got… What was the subject? Can you tell me? See, with joy they're receiving the word. Praise God.

But listen,

yet hath he not root in himself.

He didn't sit still long enough for the word to go deep down within,

> *but dureth for a while: for when tribulation or persecution ariseth because of the word, by and by he is offended.*

Don't want to go through, get angry at God and anybody else is talking to him about what God's will is.

> *He also that received seed among the thorns is he that heareth the word; and the care of this world,*

of this world…

> *and the deceitfulness of riches,*

the deceitfulness of riches.

> *choke the word,*

meaning the word was found in each one of their hearts!

> *and he becometh unfruitful,*

because the word was choked out of them.

> *But he that received seed into the good ground is he that heareth the word, and understandeth it; which also beareth fruit,*

See, when the word of God is understood by you, you're going to bring forth fruit, and we're going to go into this, the fruit business.

> *some an hundredfold, some sixty, some thirty.*

And he goes on to tell us about the kingdom of heaven, how it is sown. He also says in the word of God, when a person is cleansed of devils, that were cast out of that individual, the devils leave, they come back, especially the leader, and would look into that house and see it swept and garnished and he will go back and gather unto himself seven more demons worse than he himself and would come back and enter into that individual. Why?

Because even though they were cleansed from their sins, they failed to be filled with the Holy Spirit and to go after the fruit of the Holy Spirit. Many eyes are on the gifts, being used of God, but we'd better consider how we are receiving God with them. In the house of God, there are so many ugly things going on.

You see people beautifully used of God, but you get close to them, and you'll find out that they're a bunch of vipers. They cannot deal with you kindly, gently, lovingly, sweetly, lowly, humbly, because the fruit is not there. Back to the fifth chapter of Galatians, verse 16,

> This I say then, Walk in the Spirit, and ye shall not fulfil the lust of the flesh.

Paul is telling the Galatians that they once started out right and for a while they were growing, but he said, verse 3,

> *For I testify again to every man that is circumcised, that he is a debtor to do the whole law.*

In other words, you want to be entangled by rituals and statues of men, so that the blood is done away with? You want to be bound by this and bound by that? He said,

I testify again to every man that is circumcised, that he is a debtor to do the whole law. Christ is become of no effect unto you, whosoever of you are justified by the law; ye are fallen from grace.

For we through the Spirit wait for the hope of righteousness by faith.

We wait for the Holy Spirit to guide us in righteousness. We're to do the righteousness of God, not the works of the flesh, not the works of the law, not outward works, as so many are doing.

For in Jesus Christ neither circumcision availeth any thing, nor uncircumcision; but faith which worketh by love.

The faith of God that works by love! Not out of rituals and duties and of doctrines of men, but by the love of God motivating us to do his will. He said,

Ye did run well; who did hinder you that ye should not obey the truth? This persuasion cometh not of him that calleth you. A little leaven leaveneth the whole lump. I have confidence in you through the Lord, that ye will be none otherwise minded: but he that troubleth you shall bear his judgment, whosoever he be.

Then he says in 16,

This I say then, Walk in the Spirit, and ye shall not fulfil the lust of the flesh.

Uh-oh. We don't hear too much of this anymore.

For the flesh lusteth against the Spirit,

meaning war, wars,

and the Spirit against the flesh,

meaning the Holy Spirit wars against the flesh or the self-life, and the self-life wars against the will of the Spirit.

and these are contrary the one to the other: so that ye cannot do the things that ye would.

There is no agreement; they are at war, they are at variance with one another. There's a great division between the Holy Spirit and the self-life. That's why Jesus tells us we must deny ourselves. You heard me say earlier in the, in, in other broadcasts, did not ourselves pick up our cross and follow him because the flesh will not be subject to God. It will not be. I'll read it again, he says,

For the flesh lusteth against the Spirit, and the Spirit against the flesh: and these are contrary the one to the other: so that ye cannot do the things that ye would.

And you find that well-written in Romans 7.

But if ye be led of the Spirit, ye are not under the law.

You're not under anything of the law, of man, of rituals, and so forth. He said, if we be led by the Holy Spirit, capitalized Spirit.

Now the works

and he makes it very clear what it is,

Now the works of the flesh are manifest,

They are brought to light. Dear ones, I'm here to tell you that what's in darkness is coming to light. You can not hide it. No matter how well you guard it, it's coming out. That's the word of God, and his word stands.

> *Now the works of the flesh are manifest, which are these; Adultery, fornication, uncleanness, lasciviousness, idolatry, witchcraft, hatred, variance, emulations, wrath, strife, seditions, heresies, envyings, murders, drunkenness, revellings, and such like:*

It means more, or we would say today, etc.

> *of the which I tell you*

listen to this!

> *of the which I tell you before, as I have also told you in time past, that they which do such things shall not inherit the kingdom of God*

Is he ministering to believers or just outright rank sinners? He's talking to those of the so-called household of faith. Because the works of the flesh are brought into the house of God. And that's why we must take the word of God daily and deny ourselves with the Word.

I die daily because we read the word and we see what God is after. And if you really love your soul, you who are listening, take each word that is written here, adultery, fornication, and the like, and seek the meaning out. You may think you know the meaning, seek it out, and see whether you are in the faith.

You've got to do this because if you don't do it for yourself, allowing the Holy Spirit to guide you and direct you in the truth, don't you know you're not going to have time when Jesus appears to get right, to get these things out of your spirit? Hallelujah. And I'm talking to you, believers. I'm raised up by God to talk to believers this way, to show you the truth, no matter what you call me.

You're going to answer to God for what you hear this vessel say. Because I'm sold out to God to tell you the truth. I don't look to your offerings and your pledges. You've never heard me ask. That's up to you. God pays the bills.

He touches somebody and pays the bills. So I'm obligated to God to tell you the truth. Now he says, let me read this part again,

> *They which do such things shall not inherit the kingdom of God.*

He said,

> *but the fruit of the spirit is love.*

You love God more than anything on the face of this earth. And if you love God, you're going to love that which God loves.

The fruit of the Spirit is

> *joy,*

joy, joy. The fruit of the Spirit is

peace.

The fruit of the Spirit is

> *long suffering, gentleness, goodness, faith,
> meekness, temperance against such, there is no law.*
>
> *And they that are Christ's*

They that have known the anointed one and are following him daily,

> *have crucified the flesh with the affections and lusts.*

See, the affection comes from the old man, loving these ungodly things.

> *And they that are Christ's have crucified the flesh
> with the affections and lusts. If we live in the Spirit,*

If we say we are in the spirit of God, let us also walk in the spirit. Don't let old self be showing, deny yourself, reckon him dead.

> *If we live in the Spirit, let us also walk in the
> Spirit. Let us not be desirous of vain glory,
> provoking one another, envying one another.*

Praise the Lord of hosts. Hallelujah. Here's something that the Lord had put upon my heart to read to you. It's titled, tell them:

> Tell them who I am. I am Jesus, the Lord of heaven
> and earth. Tell them I have come to set them free
> from the yoke of bondage and sin.

Tell them there remains no more excuse for the things that they do. For I have given them power. I have given the power to set man free.

I have given my word. My word is power. I have come that all men might be set free from the yoke of bondage. Tell them to look to me. I am the deliverer. I am the one who brings salvation, for I am salvation.

They must believe. I am the Christ indeed. Who shall stand before me? Who shall allow my holy anointing to break every yoke? Who shall allow me to set them free? Yea, everyone that believeth and comes to me, said the Lord, shall know of my holy anointing and shall be liberated from themselves unto me.

For I am anointed to do these things in their lives. I am the anointed one. Is there any other savior who can set free other than me? There'd be no other savior, saith the Lord.

Tell them time is running out. I am calling my own sheep unto me, and my sheep know my voice. Those that are mine, I am drawing closer to me.

For this is the time that they come closer. Come, come closer unto me, for I am calling you to a closer relationship. Come, come closer, for I shall soon pour out my wrath on an ungodly and disobedient world, saith the Lord.

Hearken, time is running out. The end of all things is at hand. And the scripture says, but the end of all things is at hand.

Be therefore sober and watch unto prayer. (1st Peter 4 verse 7.)

The Lord gave me this sometime ago, entitled, Tell Them we've distributed this in different parts of the world and yet this has been distributed because God means business with us. It is time to take God seriously. Time is running out. Find yourself in the presence of God and do his will joyously. He's waiting for you to bear fruit.

In Jesus name, amen.

A Pillar

God bless you, everyone, for tuning in to God's holy mountain broadcast. We give God the glory and the honor that's due unto him in Jesus name. And I thank God for the opportunity to come your way again and to minister the word of God as the Holy Spirit gives utterance. God bless you, each one who has been praying for us and has been in touch with us by mail. We thank God for you. Thank God for your prayers and your support.

And I shall ask that you would continue to pray for us, that we would be faithful to do the will of God. These are trying times, but God is greater than anything and everything. And unto him we look. God bless you. Amen. Let us pray.

Father, we thank you for the opportunity that you have given us to call upon your name. And in your name, Lord Jesus, we come before the throne of grace. We're looking unto you, Father, by your spirit to give us utterance, anointing, and the wisdom and power of God to make known thy word, to make known that which is on your mind for us, the children of men. We are yours.

We are bought with the blood of Jesus Christ. And we thank you for that blood that was shed for us and all that you desire of us, the pleasure that you're looking for in us, the glory and the honor that you want us to give you. We know that it comes only from you working your mighty work in us.

Let thy word fall on good ground this day. Let the power of your word penetrate, Lord, every hindrance, every darkness, rooting up and overthrowing, casting out everything that would offend you, and let your glorious word fall richly upon good ground that we might bring forth the fruit that you're looking for and that you are requiring of us.

We ask these petitions in the name of Jesus Christ and bind the adversary on every side that would come to steal your word as it comes forth. Bind the enemy. We bind you on every side, wicked one, and we command the word of God to fall on good ground.

I will be done father as in heaven. So in earth and we give you the glory and the honor that's due unto your name. Amen.

In the third chapter of the book of Revelation, and also I'll be going back to first Corinthians 15. But in the third chapter of the book of Revelation, it reads,

> *And unto the angel of the church in Sardis write; These things saith he that hath the seven Spirits of God, and the seven stars; I know thy works, that thou hast a name that thou livest, and art dead. Be watchful, and strengthen the things which remain, that are ready to die:*

That little bit of spiritual life that is left in you and is ready to die. Be watchful and strengthen that which is still alive in you.

That comes from God. He's talking to Christians. He's talking to the church of the living God; God knows us. So, (some may say) well, that was a long time ago, but it's written here. God saw fit to see to it that the word of God would be written down for our reproof, for doctrine that we might be edified, that we might stand corrected, that we might be encouraged to go on, to follow on, to know the Lord.

God deals with His people personally, and he deals with us many times collectively. People are the same in every generation. It's just greater sins because they're greater people.

But as the preacher said in the book of Ecclesiastes, there's nothing new under the sun, and it's the truth. God knows the heart of every one of us. And when he, by his Spirit, tells John to write, write to the different churches, the seven churches. These churches that had the word of God sent to them then represent us today throughout the world. Every child of God… we belong to God. And the Lord is telling us how to overcome, how to have the victory, how to be honest in our walk with him or in our failing to walk with him, to be honest.

And this is why he's saying in the second verse, be watchful and strengthen that, strengthen the things which remain that are ready to die.

for I have not found thy works perfect before God.

They're not as I desire…

Oh, how God knows the heart of every one of us. So that knocks every excuse out in left field. God knows us, and no one's perfect, but God is, His Holy Spirit is, and Jesus, the savior of all mankind, is. And Jesus upheld the word of God when he walked here in the flesh.

He said, be holy, for your Father in heaven is holy. It is written, he said, and God is saying, be perfect. And that, that God tells you to do and that, that God requires of each one of us, God said, carry it out to the fullest extent, carry it through. That's what he means by perfection. That which you know to do, do it. Whatever God says, do it!

Remember therefore how thou hast received

He wants us to remember. Many times you say, I don't want to remember, (and quote) "Forgetting those things which are…"

Oh, how we can call on that scripture to make excuses for our little feeble ways! But Jesus is coming, He's coming for church without spot or wrinkle, without any fault, without any blemish, without any failure. And this is why Jesus, the resurrected Christ, revealing himself to John on the Isle of Patmos, as he was caught up in the spirit before the living God, is saying, remember, therefore, how thou hast received and heard and hold fast.

So we got to take inventory of how we hear things, how we hear the word of God, how we receive it. And also to hold fast to what we hear. And then he says,

and repent.

When we hear the word of God, we can't help but repent when we are not in his will. We can't cover up our sins and say, oh, I have no fault, I haven't done anything wrong. When the Holy Spirit is speaking, repent. This is why Paul says in 1 Corinthians, I die daily.

The more he heard the word, the more the word of God was revealed to him. Remember, the word of God is power. It's power. It's power to deliver. It's power to sever the connections of the self-life and everything hindering the spiritual life. It's able to do it, it's sharp. God's word is sharp, and it's mighty, piercing asunder, cutting asunder those things that are holding us back and delivering us unto God to keep the word of God, to hear it, and to hold fast to it and repent for even falling away from it. This is the kind of honest ground God is looking for.

This is how the word of God is sown and grows in us because the heart is honest when the spirit of God speaks. But here's the son of God. And see, look in verse one,

> *These things saith he that hath the seven Spirits of God,*

And they're in operation today,

> *and the seven stars.*

He's holding it all. Jesus Christ, all the power and all the glory has been delivered unto the Son of God because he was faithful to carry out the will of God even unto death. Praise his holy name.

And that's why he's telling the church of Sardis or anyone today. Verse three,

If you will not watch… We have to watch, we got to watch the way we got to watch what comes out of our mouth. We got to watch what comes against us. We got to watch against the temptations that the enemy would throw at us. We got to watch the subtle attacks. We have to watch unto prayer.

That's not a threat, that's fact. God will deal with us according to our ways.

Thou, meaning you, you have a few names,

Our garments, which is the righteousness of God, we're clothed in the righteousness of God, washed in the blood. And he's making a difference. This is in the church. He's making a difference. Some of you have, have fallen from the grace of God, but he says also concerning some, that's the fairness. That's the justice of God.

They are worthy. So don't cop a plea, (and say) Lord, I am not worthy. You can become worthy just by obeying the word of God. And this is our responsibility as citizens of the kingdom of heaven.

And then he adds,

> *He that overcometh, the same shall be clothed in white raiment; and I will not blot out his name out of the book of life, but I will confess his name before my Father, and before his angels.*

Don't you want Jesus to represent you before the Father and before that great company of angels? Hallelujah, who have watched over the children of men ever since man was established on the earth. Angels, the ministering flames of fire that God sends on our behalf from time to time. They watch us. They watch our behavior, they watch the things we do. Praise God in the highest. And Jesus will confess us even before them. If we overcome our failures and overcome our sins. I'll read it again,

> *He that overcometh, the same shall be clothed in white raiment*

The righteousness of God. Don't put it all on Jesus. You've got to do his righteousness. I've got to do his righteousness. We have to perform it.

> *and I will not blot out his name out of the book of life, but I will confess his name before my Father, and before his angels. He that hath an ear, let him hear what the Spirit saith unto the churches.*

And the Spirit is speaking today. The Spirit of God is in all
the world, bringing souls unto Jesus Christ and
strengthening souls that have already come to Jesus. Amen.
But we are to hear what he has to say and obey.

> *And to the angel of the church in Philadelphia
> write; These things saith he that is holy, he that is
> true, he that hath the key of David, he that openeth,
> and no man shutteth; and shutteth, and no man
> openeth;*

I'll open the door, and no man can close it. No man can shut
that door that I open. And I'll shut the door, and no man can
open it. I'll open the door. No man can shut it. What is he
saying?

He is the power. He is the almighty victor over all the
world, and all power and all authority has been given unto
him. He hath the key of David. Hallelujah.

> *I know thy works:*

 He's watching us as he did the church in Philadelphia.

> *I know thy works: behold, I have set before thee an
> open door,*

Thank God for the open door!

> *and no man can shut it:*

What goodness.

> *for thou hast a little strength,*

a little strength…

Meaning no matter how the enemy came to beat vehemently against you, you wouldn't take down. You maintained the little strength you had. And I have set before you an open door, and no man can shut it because you've kept my word. You've obeyed my word. You did that, which I required, and you're still performing it. And you have not denied my name. You've exalted my name, all that I am, all that I stand for; I'm holy. I'm true. And you have presented that before everyone as a witness.

I've watched you, and you have an open door and no man can slam it in your face. Hallelujah. What I've blessed you with… It's yours. Stand continually upon my word because you have not denied me.

Many have denied the Lord for the things that have come against them. They've said, like the 70, who can receive this saying? We cannot receive it, we don't understand it. When Jesus said, you have to eat of my body and drink of my blood. Meaning we've got to go through, in the life flowing power of Jesus Christ. No matter what comes against you, you will not take down. You will stand the test of time. You will not deny my name.

The 70 said, who can bear it? Do you understand what he's saying? And they turned and left from following Jesus Christ. And there are many like that today. But Jesus said, Philadelphia church, you have not denied me.

That reminds me of this place. Praise Power and Prayer Temple. Seven Oak Place, Montclair. So much has come against us from time to time. We've had warlocks and witches sitting amongst us, and God, by his power, has come against the church of Satan that he's secretly planted within us, amongst us. And when God finished dealing with them, they acknowledged what they were sent here to do, which was to take down the ministry and to see Ichabod written across the door.

But the devil is a liar! We stayed faithful! We wouldn't deny His name! We still say God is holy and live accordingly. We still say God is true and believe it with all our hearts.

All kinds of trials and tribulations have come against us. And it has amazed me to see the power of God upon this work. And we are not just here ministering the word of God on this station, but we're in different parts of this world.

This voice, this handmaidens' voice of God, is going throughout the world, proclaiming the gospel of Jesus Christ. But we have a little strength, and we have not denied God, and God has not denied us. Praise His holy name. The Lord said,

> *Behold, I will make them of the synagogue of Satan,*
> *which say they are Jews, and are not, but do lie;*

They say they belong to God. They say they are children of God. They say they are the chosen of God, but they do lie.

> *behold, I will make them to come and worship*
> *before thy feet, and to know that I have loved thee.*

We've seen God do it right here. We've seen God make them come back and acknowledge that God is in us. Hallelujah.

And our names are written out on lampposts (for the world to see). You name it. It's out there from the government on down, but to God, be the glory, to God, be the praise. God is the authority in this ministry. And we worship him. We adore him. Hallelujah.

There are things that I have taken. I said I would die before I take, but I have taken those things, and I've cast them upon the love of Jesus Christ. And the Lord has sustained me and strengthened me. And those that have stood with me in the gospel of Jesus Christ, not within this church only, but those that stand with me in different parts of the world. And God is blessing them. Hallelujah.

Because I promise God, he entrusted his word unto me, and that word will go forth as he gives it to me and not as anyone dictates to me. Glory to God. He said,

> *Behold, I will make them of the synagogue of Satan, which say they are Jews, and are not, but do lie; behold, I will make them to come and worship before thy feet, and to know that I have loved thee. Because thou hast kept the word of my patience, I also will keep thee from the hour of temptation, which shall come upon all the world, to try them that dwell upon the earth.*

It's coming, that great hour of tribulation is coming. Hallelujah. But he said, because thou hast kept the word of my patience.

He said in your patience possess your souls. When tribulations come, it requires patience to wait on God to bring us through and to strengthen us in that tribulation, in that mighty test, in that fiery furnace.

> *Behold, I come quickly: hold that fast which thou hast, that no man take thy crown.*

You hold it. No matter what is said about you. No, no matter what is done against you, hold fast to that which I have given you. Hold fast to it, that no man take that crown.

Don't you allow any person used by the devil to take the crown of life from you! That's what Jesus is saying.

> *Him that overcometh will I make a pillar*

P-I-L-L-A-R,

> *in the temple of my God,*

This is a promise!

> *and he shall go no more out: and I will write upon him the name of my God, and the name of the city of my God, which is new Jerusalem, which cometh down out of heaven from my God:*

It's coming. Hallelujah!

> *and I will write upon him my new name. He that hath an ear, let him hear what the Spirit saith unto the churches.*

He's talking to us, to the churches, not just to the church of Philadelphia, but to the churches, plural. Praise the living God. Overcome! That which you have, stand fast in it.

God's talking. He that hath an ear, let him hear. God wants to make us a pillar, amen, that's a supporter, one that undergirds, one that is given the authority and the power to be a strength, to be of steadfast faith in the work of Jesus Christ and in his kingdom, New Jerusalem.

Hallelujah. We shall be as the Lord has commended, as he has promised. In 1st Corinthians 15, verse 57,

> *But thanks be to God, which giveth us the victory through our Lord Jesus Christ.*

We have the victory.

> *Therefore, my beloved brethren, be ye stedfast, unmoveable, always abounding in the work of the Lord, forasmuch as ye know that your labour is not in vain in the Lord.*

You've got to know it. No matter what the trial may be, you've got to know it in your spirit. A pillar means to stand firm. And the Lord is telling us to hold fast. In Hebrews chapter 2, he says in verse 17,

> *Wherefore in all things it behoved him to be made like unto his brethren, that he might be a merciful and faithful high priest in things pertaining to God, to make reconciliation for the sins of the people. For in that he himself hath suffered being tempted, he is able to succour them that are tempted.*

He is able to strengthen us when temptations come against us. And this is what he talked about in Revelation. Not succumbing to temptation, but overcoming temptation by Him that was tempted, yet knew no sin. Because he says in chapter 4, verse 15,

> *For we have not an high priest which cannot be touched with the feeling of our infirmities; but was in all points tempted like as we are, yet without sin.*

He didn't succumb to it. And we can trust him to keep us from succumbing to sin.

> *Let us therefore come boldly unto the throne of grace, that we may obtain mercy, and find grace to help in time of need.*

Come boldly when you're tempted. Come boldly to the throne of grace. Come in the name of Jesus before the Father's throne and trust the Lord God to strengthen you, to secure you, to give you added power, to give you added strength, to give you added wisdom and knowledge to defeat the enemy because Christ Jesus has defeated him. And we're to stand firm in what Christ has accomplished for us in Jesus name.

God bless you. Amen.

Blameless I

First Aired May 21ˢᵗ, 2000

Pray with me, and as we're getting ready to pray, be sure you have your Bibles with you. I love for the people that are listening to read along with me as we read the Word of God, that you might see for yourself what God is saying, because indeed we shall all answer before the judgment seat of Christ concerning the Word of God, what we have believed and what we have done with the Word of God. This is why the gospel is preached, that we may be quickened to know that we are accountable for the Word of God. Amen. Let us pray.

Precious Father, before the throne of grace, we come once more and again in the authoritative name of Jesus. We're asking, Lord God, as the Word of God goes forth today, that Thy will shall be done, and Thy plan for Thy people may be made known to all that are listening.

Bless your people today. Bless the Word of God as it goes forth into the heart and the minds of Thy people, and let the Word of God find good ground, fruitful ground, that it may grow thereby and cause Thy people to triumph in the knowledge and in the grace of the living God, and in the knowledge of Jesus Christ, whom Thou hast sent to be our Savior, to be our Lord, and to be our friend.

Have mercy upon those, O God, that do not know You today. Draw them by Thy Spirit as the Word of God is being ministered. Bring unto You, O God, by Thy power and by Thy Holy Spirit. In Jesus' name we pray, saved to the uttermost, we pray, amen and amen.

The Word of God, found in the first chapter of Luke. We'll begin reading from the very first verse,

> *Forasmuch as many have taken in hand to set forth in order a declaration of those things which are most surely believed among us, even as they delivered them unto us, which from the beginning were eyewitnesses, and ministers of the word;*

This is Luke, the great physician, writing to the people as he heard the gospel and he wrote it down, those things that he heard and believed of those that knew Jesus Christ personally, that handled Him, that walked with Him, that were taught three years by the Lord Jesus Christ. And that's why it's important for us, when we hear the Word, to believe also. I'll read verse two again. He said,

> *even as they delivered them unto us, which from the beginning were eyewitnesses, and ministers of the word; it seemed good to me also, having had perfect understanding of all things from the very first, to write unto thee in order, most excellent Theophilus, that thou mightest know the certainty of those things, wherein thou hast been instructed.*

And that's the will of God for each one of us, that we might know the certainty of the things whereby we have been taught from the Word of God. There are many things going out that are not sound, and they're not steadfast. It's not the ground of the truth that God has given us, but we are to know what the truth really is.

And without knowing the truth, Jesus Christ says, I am the way, the truth, and the life. We must know Him in order to understand the written Word. We must know the living Word. And this is what Luke is testifying and writing to those and to us today. Amen. Those in his day and the Holy Spirit saw to it that his words were kept, that we might also say, yea, Lord. Amen.

He says, verse five,

> *There was in the days of Herod, the king of Judœa, a certain priest named Zacharias, of the course of Abia: and his wife was of the daughters of Aaron, and her name was Elisabeth. And they were both righteous before God, walking in all the commandments and ordinances of the Lord blameless.*

And that's the title of this message today, blameless. This couple was walking in all the ways that they had been instructed in the way of the Lord God, and they kept it perfectly. They were blameless.

And they had no child, because Elisabeth was barren, and they both were *now* well stricken in years.

> *And it came to pass, that while he executed the priest's office before God in the order of his course, according to the custom of the priest's office, his lot was to burn incense when he went into*

*the temple of the Lord. And the whole multitude of
the people were praying without at the time of
incense.*

*And there appeared unto him an angel of the Lord
standing on the right side of the altar of
incense. And when Zacharias saw him, he was
troubled, and fear fell upon him. But the angel said
unto him, Fear not, Zacharias: for thy prayer is
heard; and thy wife Elisabeth shall bear thee a son,
and thou shalt call his name John. And thou shalt
have joy and gladness; and many shall rejoice at his
birth.*

*For he shall be great in the sight of the Lord, and
shall drink neither wine nor strong drink; and he
shall be filled with the Holy Ghost, even from his
mother's womb. And many of the children of Israel
shall he turn to the Lord their God. And he shall go
before him in the spirit and power of Elias, to turn
the hearts of the fathers to the children, and the
disobedient to the wisdom of the just; to make ready
a people prepared for the Lord.*

That was the ministry of John the Baptist. In Malachi, the
prophet Malachi prophesied of John the Baptist. He didn't
call him by name, but he said he would be in the spirit of
Elijah, Elias, meaning Elijah. Elijah was a man of fire,
speaking to all Israel the word of God with power and with
might, with strength, in the passion of the Spirit of God.

And so that mantle actually fell upon John the Baptist, even while his mother Elizabeth was carrying him. John the Baptist was filled with the Holy Ghost, even from his mother's womb, according to Luke 1 verse 15. And that's important to note, because at that time the Holy Spirit was not freely given upon everyone as it is today.

Glory to God. Joah, too, had not fully been fulfilled, the prophecy of Joel, the prophet Joel. In the last days, I shall pour out my Spirit upon all flesh, my sons and daughters, and I emphasize, and daughters, shall prophesy. Glory to God.

But this was a special work of grace, a special work of the Holy Spirit to fill John with the Holy Ghost, even from his mother's womb, because there was a mighty work set forth for him to do, to go before Jesus Christ, before the ministry of Jesus Christ was made public, and to prepare the hearts of those that would receive the Lord Jesus as their Savior.

Now John went forth ministering, saying, prepare your hearts. And he would speak against the vipers, those who were ignorant of the will of God and certainly did not know or want to know the will of God. And he said, you generation of vipers who hath warned you to flee the wrath to come, meaning the wrath of God that is coming against and upon the disobedient of the earth, that day shall also come.

God is moving now in certain places, but God shall pour out His wrath upon every disobedient person in that last day.

Glory to God. And so John goes forth. He's a forerunner of the gospel of Jesus Christ, preparing the hearts, baptizing them unto repentance of their sins, that they might be in readiness to receive the gospel that Jesus Christ would be speaking from the heart of the Father in heaven.

This is so important to understand why the Holy Ghost was given to John before he was actually born. Amen. When Mary told Elizabeth, her cousin, of her being pregnant or carrying the Lord Jesus in her womb, the baby leaped in Elizabeth's womb for joy because God was doing a mighty thing in little John the Baptist in his mother's womb. Hallelujah.

But we, the preachers and teachers of this hour, and have been from the time that the gospel was being preached of old, are actually doing the same work. Jesus is coming again… He's coming on a cloud; He's not coming to the earth at that time. He's coming on a cloud to receive all who are ready, all who are prepared for His coming. And this is why I named this particular broadcast blameless. We are to be blameless before God in that day.

Many have evil things to say of the Holy Spirit because of unbelief. And some, not speaking evil, but in ignorance, thinking that because many do not speak in a heavenly language, that it doesn't matter. We all are filled with the Spirit. That's not particularly the truth.

We all are born into the kingdom of God by the Spirit of God. We must be born again, and it is by the Spirit of God. But there is a greater measure of grace, a greater measure of power that God longs to give the church of Jesus Christ.

And that is the baptism of the Holy Ghost. That's why Jesus came. He came to baptize us with fire, as He did on the initial day of Pentecost.

But that work of grace didn't subside then. God is still moving by His Spirit. There was a time when Paul came into Ephesus, and he asked the people, and it's found in Acts, the 19th chapter, let me read it.

I'll start at the very first verse, Acts 19.

> *And it came to pass, that, while Apollos was at Corinth, Paul having passed through the upper coasts came to Ephesus: and finding certain disciples, he said unto them, Have ye received the Holy Ghost since ye believed? And they said unto him, We have not so much as heard whether there be any Holy Ghost.*
>
> *And he said unto them, Unto what then were ye baptized? And they said, Unto John's baptism. Then said Paul, John verily baptized with the baptism of repentance, saying unto the people, that they should believe on him which should come after him, that is, on Christ Jesus. When they heard this, they were baptized in the name of the Lord Jesus.*
>
> *And when Paul had laid his hands upon them, the Holy Ghost came on them; and they spake with tongues, and prophesied. And all the men were about twelve.*

What God is saying here, and we see other evidence of things like this happening in the book of Acts, the Acts of the Holy Ghost, and He is still in action today, today, the same Holy Ghost, the same Holy Spirit, the same power of God, the same anointing, this fire of God, the Spirit of truth.

The church of Jesus Christ must awake and put on the strength of God, and it's not just by our will only, it's by the power of God.

One phrase in the Word of God, it's not by might nor by power, but by my Spirit, said the Lord, has been underestimated. God wants us to know the power of God in this last day. We are to be equipped and matchless against the works of the devil.

We are to be full of the power of God, and that power comes from the Spirit of the Most High God. This is how the people were blameless. This is how Elizabeth and Zacharias, the high priest, were blameless because they were kept by the Holy Spirit. They were kept by the power of God.

And if we are to be blameless at the appearing of Jesus Christ, we are to be filled with the unction of the Holy Spirit. He is the one who will render us blameless at the appearing of Jesus Christ when He comes, to gather the elect unto Himself. Amen.

In the first chapter of the first Corinthians, the Word of God tells us, I'll read from the first verse all the way down to eight. I'm just taking my time here because I want you to see clearly why we need to ask the Lord to fill us with the Holy Ghost. We need this, and one experience is not enough.

We need a daily, we need a continual flow and a baptism of the Holy Spirit to equip us for that day, for this day. And if the Lord says to spare us until tomorrow, we need to ask again, Lord, flood my soul, flood my soul. We need to be speaking in heavenly language daily that we might stay equipped for the test that awaits us, for the trials that await us, for the wars that come against us.

That we might be blameless, that we might be steadfast and unmovable until Jesus comes for us. In the very first verse, First Corinthians chapter 1, Paul says,

> *Paul, called to be an apostle of Jesus Christ*
> *through the will of God, and*
> *Sosthenes our brother, unto the church of God*
> *which is at Corinth, to them that are sanctified in*
> *Christ Jesus, called to be saints, with all that in*
> *every place call upon the name of Jesus Christ our*
> *Lord, both their's and our's: grace be unto you, and*
> *peace, from God our Father, and from the Lord*
> *Jesus Christ.*

> *I thank my God always on your behalf, for the grace*
> *of God which is given you by Jesus Christ; that in*
> *every thing ye are enriched by him, in all utterance,*
> *and in all knowledge;*

You see why we have to be filled through and through… a continual work of the Holy Spirit? This is the will of God,

> *for the grace of God which is given you by Jesus*
> *Christ; that in every thing ye are enriched by him,*
> *in all utterance, and in all knowledge; even as the*
> *testimony of Christ was confirmed in you: so that ye*

See? That you come behind in no gift! That we may be found with the operations of the gifts of the Holy Spirit, knowledge, wisdom, amen, all of these things… miracles, the ministry of miracles, healings, all of these things that God has for the church in this day. God does not want us to come behind in anything, and we will not, if we allow the Holy Spirit to have free course within us; it's up to our will, glory to His name. He says,

> so that ye come behind in no gift; waiting for the coming of our Lord Jesus Christ: who shall also confirm you unto the end,

Christ confirming us unto the end,

> that ye may be blameless in the day of our Lord Jesus Christ.

That day is coming and it's soon precious ones, it is soon, glory to God, just as the enemy, satan, the enemy of all the souls of mankind is ordaining and anointing his prophets and his priests to do the ungodly, to work abominations, to destroy, to kill, to maim, to make ill, to keep back from the light, from walking in the light, to keep back from the knowledge of who Jesus is.

He's doing it, and his work has increased; everywhere you look, there are many works of evil popping up over the air, over the airwaves, by television, glory be to God, by computers, you name it, by satellites, the works of the enemy increasing to even destroy the little ones, to maim their minds with witchcrafts in every form. And these things are coming out over and over in greater numbers, in greater quantities, in greater anointing of the devil's evil works.

How much more shall we, the believers of Jesus Christ, those that are called by his name, should be empowered to overthrow and to cast down, to bind up and cast out the works of the devil, we must be filled with the Holy Ghost and Power. That we might remain blameless because great temptations are coming against the church of Jesus Christ as never before.

If we are not walking in the Holy Spirit, obedient to the will of God, following the instructions that only the Holy Ghost can bring unto us and guide us into, we are going to be full of fault and full of disobedience because one act of disobedience will maim the work of God in us.

We must be blameless, and we cannot do it ourselves; our faith alone cannot stand. We must have the faith of God, and we must stand in the power of the Holy Spirit in order to combat the evil forces. Remember Jesus said, when you pray, say, deliver us from evil, and then at the end of that prayer, he says, for thine is the kingdom and the power, see, that's what God wants us to know and understand, not just hear it and let it slip, but know it, be enriched in the knowledge and in the utterance that Jesus Christ would give us.

This is the will of God for us, that we might be found at his appearing without spot and without blemish. Let me read that portion of the scriptures found in 2nd Peter, the third chapter, and I'll begin at verse 10,

> *But the day of the Lord will come as a thief in the night; in the which the heavens shall pass away with a great noise, and the elements shall melt with fervent heat, the earth also and the works that are therein shall be burned up. Seeing then that all these things shall be dissolved, what manner of persons ought ye to be in all holy conversation and godliness, looking for and hasting unto the coming of the day of God, wherein the heavens being on fire shall be dissolved,*

that is the last day,

> *and the elements shall melt with fervent heat? Nevertheless we, according to his promise, look for new heavens and a new earth, wherein dwelleth righteousness.*
>
> *Wherefore, beloved, seeing that ye look for such things, be diligent that ye may be found of him in peace, without spot, and blameless.*

Now this he is speaking of at the very last day when the Lord comes to take vengeance on the earth, but there is another day before that last day where the Lord will rapture or catch up his church, his body, his bride that are watching and waiting and prepared for his appearing Jesus tells us in Matthew 24 that when the bride is caught up, those that have been watching and waiting and have made themselves ready by seeing that their lamps are full of oil and burning.

Glory to God, when he comes for his bride, he will shut the door. And the five foolish virgins, he gives us in the parable, will come seeking and knocking on that door because they were not prepared, and they had to go and buy oil for themselves. And when the door was shut, they came seeking to enter, and the Lord told them, I know you not, I know you not.

You see? We are to be known of God most intimately, we are to be known of God, and we are to know him most intimately. And who can do that except the Holy Spirit in us, so seek the baptism, don't let anyone tell you it is not for you today. We are to pray in the Spirit; we are to pray in tongues that only the Holy Spirit can give us. It is important to know this; it is most important to know this.

In the third chapter of Philippians, let me see, I think I'll begin at the sixth verse, yes, Paul is talking about,

> *concerning zeal, persecuting the church; touching the righteousness which is in the law, blameless.*

What Paul did according to the law of Moses, he did with all his heart, even though he was dead wrong, but he did it according to the zeal and the knowledge that he had. But that knowledge was not enough because he didn't know Jesus Christ; he had not met Jesus personally.

And this is the example that is set here in the Word of God for us to know, to realize that we have to know this Jesus personally, that we do not do havoc to the believers of Jesus Christ, amen.

Many have been persecuted because they believe in the
baptism of the Holy Ghost with fire, let God's will be done
today in you, amen and amen.

Blameless II

First Aired June 4th, 2000

Praise God in the highest. We thank the Lord for the opportunity once more and again that he has given us to come your way again. The Lord God is perfect, and this is why we are here: to show forth his perfection and what he desires in the saints that he has redeemed in the earth.

We are his body, the workmanship of his glory, and God expects great things, amen, great things from us. All the mighty things that he's put within our being, God expects to receive the fruit thereof, and this is why the word of God is so important.

Let us go to the book of Colossians. It's in the New Testament, and let us read… chapter 1 of the book of Colossians,

> *Paul, an apostle of Jesus Christ by the will of God, and Timotheus our brother, to the saints and faithful brethren in Christ which are at Colosse:*
> *Grace be unto you, and peace, from God our Father and the Lord Jesus Christ.*
>
> *We give thanks to God and the Father of our Lord Jesus Christ, praying always for you, since we heard of your faith in Christ Jesus, and of the love which ye have to all the saints, for the hope which is laid up for you in heaven, whereof ye heard before in the word of the truth of the gospel; which*

*is come unto you, as it is in all the world; and
bringeth forth fruit, as it doth also in you, since the
day ye heard of it, and knew the grace of God in
truth:*

*as ye also learned of Epaphras our dear
fellowservant, who is for you a faithful minister of
Christ; who also declared unto us your love in the
Spirit.*

*For this cause we also, since the day we heard it, do
not cease to pray for you, and to desire that ye
might be filled with the knowledge of his will in all
wisdom and spiritual understanding; that ye might
walk worthy of the Lord unto all pleasing, being
fruitful in every good work, and increasing in the
knowledge of God;*

What the Lord is really saying here through the apostle
Paul that wrote this epistle or this letter, the Lord's will, the
Lord God's will is that we might walk worthy of the Lord,
worthy of the Lord Jesus Christ, you see, unto all pleasing.
See, that's our responsibility as children of God. And God
has put within us a free will, a mind, and a heart as well as
a soul.

And it is up to us to choose what we desire to do with our
lives, whether to put it in the hands of God or choose to live
our own way. We're under one power. There are two powers
that work in this earth, the power of God and the power of
the devil.

We can only be under one, and God is telling us to choose
which one we are subject to. God will not force us; it is his

will, it is his great pleasure, it is a strong desire that we would walk under his authority, under his rule, because his heart is for us. It is for our good. His desire is that we will belong to him. He's already provided for us. He's made the way for us, but still it is ours to choose whom we shall serve. Will it be God or will it be Satan? That choice is ours.

And know and rest assuredly that whatever choice we make, it will meet us in the end. If we made God our choice, then God will own us in the end of the age, at the end of this world.

But the word of God tells us as Christians, we who are born again, that have accepted Christ Jesus as our personal savior, that we might walk worthy of the Lord unto all pleasing. And that is possible if we are following the lead of the Holy Spirit. If we are trusting in the keeping power of God to keep us from the temptations of the devil, and the lust of the flesh, and the pride of this life, we can walk unto all pleasing unto God, being fruitful in every good work and increasing in the knowledge of God.

See, it's more than just being born again. When we are first born again into the kingdom of God, we're newborn babes. And as newborn babes, we desire the sincere milk of the word of God. We desire to know him. But it seems when we grow older, there is a falling away from that sincere desire.

And we are to hold firm to that which God gives us, lest at any time we let it slip. We're to be on this way with rejoicing and desiring a greater desire in our hearts to

know, to know him better in whom we believe. And his
name is Christ Jesus. He's the one who has purchased our
salvation with his own body and his own blood on that old
rugged cross. And it's God's desire, the Father who sent
Jesus Christ to redeem us, to be just as Jesus, the express
image of God, when he came here on the earth in flesh and
blood.

The word of God says in Hebrews chapter 1, verse 3,

> *who being the brightness of his glory, and the
> express image of his person, and upholding all
> things by the word of his power, when he had by
> himself purged our sins, sat down on the right hand
> of the Majesty on high;*

And that's where Jesus is right now in his glorified body,
sitting on the right hand of the majesty of God. Glory to
God. Now, just as Jesus, being the express image of the
Father before the world, so are we to be the express image
of Jesus Christ.

Isn't it marvelous that God has called us to represent the
Godhead body on this earth through the person of Jesus
Christ and his Holy Spirit? It's marvelous. And this is why
we are to walk in a spiritual way, a glorified way, an
anointed way, following hard after God. This is the will of
God for every one of us.

And in Colossians, let us finish,

> *giving thanks unto the Father, which hath made us
> meet to be partakers of the inheritance of the saints
> in light:*

Our inheritance is in the Lord God Almighty, and we are God's inheritance. It works both ways. We are joint heirs with Jesus Christ, joint heirs to receive and possess the kingdom of God, heaven, which is our home. We're pilgrims just passing through here, through this earth. Our soul knows that most grossly, hallelujah, our soul is acquainted with the thought that we are just pilgrims passing through.

This is not our home. No matter what God sees fit to bless us with while we are yet on this earth, this earth is not truly our home. Our home is in glory in the heavens. Glory to God. And one day we will come back to this earth. We will come back and reign with Jesus Christ for a thousand years.

But until then, while we are passing through the earth in Jesus name, we are to give thanks unto the Father and realize that we have been made

> *partakers of the inheritance of the saints in light: who hath delivered us from the power of darkness,*

We're delivered from Satan's dominion, and God has translated us into the kingdom of his dear Son. This is what God has done for us.

> *and hath translated us into the kingdom of his dear Son: in whom we have redemption through his blood, even the forgiveness of sins: Who is the image of the invisible God,*

You see this? I read it also in Hebrews 1 verse 3.

*for by him were all things created, that are in
heaven, and that are in earth, visible and invisible,
whether they be thrones, or dominions, or
principalities, or powers: all things were created by
him, and for him: and he is before all things, and by
him all things consist.*

He's speaking of Christ Jesus

and he is the head of the body.

We're his body, the church,

who is the beginning, the firstborn from the dead;

still speaking of Jesus,

*that in all things he might have the
preeminence. For it pleased the Father that in him
should all fulness dwell;*

God is well pleased with his son, Jesus Christ, and all
fullness, all fullness dwells in Christ.

*and, having made peace through the blood of his
cross, by him to reconcile all things unto himself; by
him, I say, whether they be things in earth, or things
in heaven.*

*And you, that were sometime alienated and enemies
in your mind by wicked works, yet now hath he
reconciled*

See, we were enemies when we went in our own way,
doing our wicked thoughts. You see, going in our own

fleshly way. But now we are reconciled to God through Jesus Christ. Hallelujah.

> *in the body of his flesh through death, to present you holy and unblameable and unreproveable in his sight:*

This is what God has perfected through Jesus Christ, in Christ, and by Christ. The body, we are his body. Everyone who has received the Lord Jesus Christ as their personal savior and crowned him Lord in their hearts, go beyond savior, and allow him to be king and Lord of our lives.

We are to be presented unto God the Father, holy and unblameable and unreprovable in his sight.

> *If,*

He says,

> *ye continue in the faith grounded and settled,*

See, there is a progression of growth. We are to progress daily. The more we learn of Jesus Christ, the more we desire to please him and walk upright before him. And it's done by his Spirit, the Holy Spirit, empowering us to live victoriously over ourselves, over the world, and over the devil. Hallelujah.

There is an enemy called self that is just as diabolical as Satan. Satan doesn't have to possess an individual's life to entice one to do wickedness. All he has to do is to appeal to the self-life. That's why Jesus said we must deny ourselves because self wants no part of the spiritual walk. Self is used to having Satan as ruler and Lord.

And self does not want and cannot do the things that God requires. That's why self must be denied. And we are to take up our position and our obligation as citizens of the kingdom of God to do those things that are well pleasing in the sight of the most high. And Jesus is praying for us. He's praying for us through. He's praying us through, that we might be victorious. He's not just sitting there and finished his work in heaven.

Jesus is yet working for us. He is yet working. Intercession is a great work; it is a tedious work. And he's watching over us as the head. We are here in this world, but we do not belong to this world. And certainly, we should not be partakers of this worldliness that we are beholding with our eyes daily. We're to be a separate people.

Word of God tells us in Peter, in 2nd Peter, that we are a royal priesthood, a peculiar people, a holy nation, while we are still on this earth. The world might call us strange, even crazy, because they do not understand the ways of God. But we, being the express image of Jesus Christ, we are made partakers of his person. And we are to show forth who Jesus is by walking in his light.

We are made lights in this world. And God is calling us to walk upright and all that we do to be pleasing and acceptable in his sight. Precious ones, this is what God has ordained for us. And if we live any less than what God has ordained, we are not living according to the will of God.

And if we are not living according to his will, then we are children of disobedience, not allowing God to have his way in us. God's way is always right. And God's way is good. God is good.

Jehovah-Jireh is good. Christ Jesus is good. And all that he is planting in us is good. And we are to manifest his goodness as we seek him daily. As I said before, there is a progression of growth. We're to grow up in Jesus. We are not to remain newborn babes.

Many would love to stay in that manner, but that's not pleasing to God. It wouldn't be right if we were to bring a child into this world… we would know something was very wrong if that child did not grow. And so it is with the kingdom of God. When a newborn babe is birthed into the kingdom of God, we act like babes.

But as we grow in the grace and in the knowledge of who Jesus is, of Jesus Christ, putting on his ways as we learn him, yielding to his authority by his Spirit, then we grow up unto him in all fullness and see it's in Christ that all fullness dwells.

I hope you understand this. God is expecting better things of all of us. It is time to quit like men. It is time to stop acting like babes. And it's time to put on the Lord Jesus Christ in full authority and allow him to rule. There are greater places that the Lord desires to take us in him while we are still on the face of this earth. Let's continue. I'll read verse 23 again,

> *if ye continue in the faith grounded and settled,*
> *and be not moved away from the hope of the gospel,*
> *which ye have heard, and which was preached to*
> *every creature which is under heaven; whereof I*

See, many of us have to suffer many things, many things
for the gospel's sake. The enemy does not want us to
proclaim the gospel of Jesus Christ as it should be. This is
no watered-down gospel; we speak the truth, the Holy
Ghost bearing us witness.

All heaven is listening to what we are saying, what we are
proclaiming to his body and to all the world concerning this
great and mighty Savior, Jesus Christ. And we must give an
account.

And because of this, the devil despises us. In the word of
God, in Ephesians, it says, let me see, Ephesians 4, verse
11,

And he gave some,

meaning the Lord Jesus Christ,

*gave some, apostles; and some, prophets; and some,
evangelists; and some, pastors and teachers; for the
perfecting of the saints,*

That means growing up as God has ordained in the grace
and in the knowledge of who he is, of Jesus Christ.

for the perfecting of the saints,

that we might be made perfect. No blame, no fault, no sin.

for the work of the ministry, for the edifying of the body of Christ: till we all come in the unity of the faith,

That's what the Spirit of God is striving for. And this is why the five, four ministries are given. It's for the perfecting of the saints. Let me read those five, four ministries. Prophets, evangelists, pastors, first apostles, then prophets, evangelists, pastors, and teachers.

All pertaining to the word of God. Proclaiming the word of God in its fullness, in its wholeness. Not just handing you milk. That's for newborn babes, and God knows they need the milk. But we that have been saved for years, we are to act our age in Christ. Hallelujah.

And God is doing a quick work now. For the coming of the Lord is very near. And we are not to act like little children, but we are to grow in the thought, in the knowledge, in the power of God. We should be increasing daily as God has ordained.

And this is not to be taken lightly. It's for the perfecting of the saints. This is why we are on radio today. To proclaim unto you what God is after… The will of God. And when we cease speaking, the Holy Spirit is yet there with you. To take you even deeper than what we say.

Praise God as you seek God's face. As you call upon His name. And ask Him to help you to grow. To help you to know who Jesus is.

It is given unto us to know. This mystery is no longer a mystery to those that know God. Let me read again in Colossians verse 25, he says,

> *whereof I am made a minister, according to the dispensation of God which is given to me for you, to fulfil the word of God; even the mystery which hath been hid from ages and from generations, but now is made manifest to his saints:*

He has brought light to us! We see, we can see clearly. It's no longer hidden.

> *to whom God would make known what is the riches of the glory of this mystery among the Gentiles; which is Christ in you, the hope of glory:*

To whom God would make known what is the riches of the glory of this mystery among the Gentiles. Which is Christ in you, the hope of glory. Where do you stand today? How close are you with Jesus Christ? Is He still a mystery to you? Or is He your loving friend whom you communicate with throughout the day and even in the night season?

Where is Jesus in your life? Are you allowing Him to work the works of God in you? Are you growing in His grace? Have you partaken of His ways? Do you know Him better than when you first accepted Him as your Savior? Where are you in Christ? Are you growing up? This is the will of God concerning you. That you grow, Hallelujah, in His grace. He is your hope. He should no longer be a mystery to you.

He should be open to you, and you open to Him.

> *to whom God would make known what is the riches
> of the glory of this mystery among the Gentiles;
> which is Christ in you, the hope of glory: whom we
> preach, warning every man, and teaching every
> man in all wisdom; that we may present every man
> perfect in Christ Jesus: whereunto I also labour,
> striving according to his working, which worketh in
> me mightily.*

This is what we ministers of the gospel have to go through.
We have to go through. And we must preach the truth.
Rightly divided. warning every person. Teaching every
person. In all wisdom. In all the wisdom of Christ Jesus.

That we may present every man without fault. Without
blame. Present every man perfect in Christ Jesus. This is
why the word of God is given daily. This is why we preach
and teach. And suffer, yes, for His name's sake, for the
gospel's sake.

That you might be edified. That you might be presented
blameless at His appearing. Blameless, precious ones, is the
will of God for you. In Jesus name. Walk upright. Do His
good pleasure. Walk unto all pleasing. Amen and amen.
God be with you, 'till we meet again.

The Way

First Aired Sept 8th, 2002

God is so good to us all the time. Bless His Holy Name, and we thank God for the richness of His Word. I love the Word of God. I thank God that He's planted in my heart, and I'm sure as many of you who are listening, you love the Word of God just as I do. The Word of God is a lamp unto our feet, and a light unto our pathway, and we're speaking from the series, The Way.

We know that Jesus Christ is that precious way that leads us to the Father, and He is the way of God completely. Not in some instances, but altogether, Christ Jesus is the way of life, indeed. And God the Father has sent Him to show us the way to please the Father. You know, we are all gifted by the grace of God.

Every man has a portion of faith. With every person, God has instilled into every man a measure of faith, but faith without knowing who God the Father is… is dead. It may be very well working on your behalf as far as the flesh is concerned or the personal desires of this world, but to please God, we must have the faith of God.

Our hearts and minds must be in tune to His will, to know His will. And this is why we are here, as God has raised up many ministers of the gospel of Jesus Christ. Praise God to bring perfection to the church, to the body of Christ. We in ourselves can do nothing, for we in ourselves know nothing of ourselves, but as we seek the face of God as His messengers, according to Malachi chapter 2, we are to hear the word from God on high through the power of the Holy Ghost, and He it is that takes that which is of the Father and reveals unto us, and we give it to you as God gives it to us.

This is the ministry, this is the five-fold ministry that works in the body of Jesus Christ today. Thank God for the five-fold ministry: apostle, prophet, evangelist, pastor, and teacher. Praise God, it's for the effectual working of God's power, His plan, with His mighty word in operation to perfect the church of Jesus. And this is why we are here, to give glory and honor to His name and to touch you with His word, even as He has touched us.

It's a marvelous privilege, and it's also great for you to be recipients of God's word. Hallelujah. In the second chapter of the book of Ephesians, please turn with me to the second chapter of the book of Ephesians, and as you're turning, let us pray.

Father, before the throne of grace, we come giving thanks to you and giving you honor and glory, giving you praise for the things that you've done in us and for us in this world. We thank you for choosing us and calling us out of this world, bringing us unto you through the person of your Son and His precious blood that He shed for us. Thank you for washing us and cleansing us from all foulness and sin.

Glory be to God. We thank you, Lord, for giving us of your nature. Praise your holy name. We thank you for sharing with us the kingdom of God and sharing with us your only begotten Son. Thank you for such honor, Lord, that you have bestowed upon us as children of men, that you will look upon us with favor, with your divine favor, and bring us into your holy presence.

Thank you for the privilege that we can approach the throne of grace in the person of Jesus Christ and in His precious name. Amen. Have your mighty way this day. Gather up the loins of our minds, each one of us, as we go into the word of God. Break the bread of life unto us and give us the grace to eat thereof.

Give us a perfect understanding to what you will have us to know. Enlighten our eyes that we might see, our ears sanctify that we might hear, and our hearts and spirits sanctify unto yourself that we might receive your engrafted word and grow thereby that we may bring forth more fruit unto you. In Jesus' precious name.

Let all opposing forces of the wicked one be bound on every side. I commend it to be so in the authoritative name of Jesus Christ. Amen and amen.

Ephesians chapter 2,

> *And you hath he quickened, who were dead in trespasses and sins; wherein in time past ye walked according to the course of this world, according to the prince of the power of the air, the spirit that now worketh in the children of disobedience:*

Let me explain what the apostle is saying here, Paul the apostle, writing unto the church at Ephesus. He's saying that we, all of us, whatever generation we have been in, and I say we, that means those who have been in other generations, and the Lord has taken home to be with him.

And even to this generation in which we are living, we, the children of God, whether they are home in glory or whether we're yet here on the face of this earth, he is speaking to us. And you hath he quickened who were dead in trespasses and sins. You see, every one of us, that's why Jesus said we must be born again.

And he says, wherein in time past, that was before we were born again, ye walked according to the course of this world, according to the course of this world. Remember that phrase, according to the prince of the power of the air. And he is talking about satan.

He is the prince and the evil power of the air. This is where he goes to and fro. And he says the spirit that now worketh in the children of disobedience, the evil spirit that causes those that will not believe God or will not submit themselves to the way of the Lord, to the righteousness of God, they are children, they're called children of disobedience.

> *among whom also we all had our conversation in times past*

…in times past. In other words, it should not be the same way because we are born again. And there is a difference in us now. We are no more children of the prince of the power of the air. We are now the children of God because we are born again.

And if anyone is listening that have not been born again by the spirit of God and washed in the blood of the lamb, Jesus Christ, this invitation is to you also.

It's time to hear the word of God and believe thereon and ask the Lord to come into your heart that the Holy Spirit can say also of you in times past, but not now. I'm going to read verse three again.

> *among whom also we all had our conversation in times past in the lusts of our flesh, fulfilling the desires of the flesh and of the mind; and were by nature the children of wrath, even as others.*

whereby nature, you see why we must be born again, that devilish nature in the self-life will be destroyed, will be broken, hallelujah. And that's the power of salvation to everyone that believe. God transforms us into the kingdom of the Most High God. And he gives us his nature, righteousness, the planting of the Lord.

So,

> *But God who is rich in mercy,*

verse four, and he is,

> *for his great love wherewith he loved us, even when we were dead in sins,*

You see, sin brings death and destruction, you see,

> *even when we were dead in sins, hath quickened us together with Christ,*

By grace, you're saved. It's the grace of God. Remember what we read to you before in one of the broadcasts? The first man, Adam, was a soul, but the second man, Adam, quickening spirit.

And this is what he means by he has quickened us. He has raised us up together. In verse five,

> *even when we were dead in sins, hath quickened us together with Christ,*

together with Christ, with Christ… We're joint heirs with Christ in the kingdom of God. Isn't it marvelous? This is why it is important for us to know Jesus, not just the blunder around saying, I believe, go beyond belief, get to know Him, for he is our dear savior. He is our constant friend indeed, and he's our help.

He's that quickening power that worketh in us. He quickens our mortal bodies as well, keeping us strong, keeping us healthy, healthy in the things of God, keeping our feet from falling. And look what we have working for us.

We have God's grace. We have God's great love. We have his gift from on high, salvation through Jesus Christ, the precious blood that he shed for us. We have the Holy Spirit empowering us, living within us, guiding us, and sealing us. We have the angelic host of God working on our behalf, the administering angels, and flames of fire. And they're sent from the throne of God from time to time to come here in this earth and minister to us according as our needs should be.

And we have the prayers of the dear saints of God on this earth, the prayers of the righteous watching and going up before the throne of God on our behalf. Oh, we are enriched indeed by the power of God. The Lord Jesus has not left us alone.

He is ever with us. And we must come into that, that acknowledgement, and we must put into practice daily that the Lord has provided for us these great provisions that he has made for us, and take it, receive it daily, consciously, knowing that he is the same today as he was yesterday.

Just as he was concerning the patriarchs of old who have gone on to their rest, he is that same God over us working in such a mighty and glorious way in us today. Bless his holy name. Let your mind be elevated to think on these things constantly, being made aware. And the Holy Spirit's job is to keep us mindful of who we are serving and what he is in our lives.

Verse six, and have raised us up together and made us together to sit together in heavenly places in Christ Jesus. Verse six again,

> *and hath raised us up together, and made us sit together in heavenly places in Christ Jesus:*

in heavenly places, far above the principalities and powers of the air, where satan's dominion is. Praise God!

> *that in the ages to come he might shew the exceeding riches of his grace in his kindness toward us through Christ Jesus.*

Now, just think on the years that have passed, the hundreds of years that have passed since this epistle was written. See where Paul is coming from. He said that in the ages to come, and many ages have passed, and we are in that hour that he is speaking of. He says

> *that in the ages to come he might shew the exceeding riches of his grace in his kindness toward us through Christ Jesus.*

And remember what he wrote also, that I have not seen, neither have the ear heard the good things that the Lord hath in store for them that love him. He said, but they are revealed unto us by his Spirit. Praise his holy name!

So it is of utmost importance that our eyes, the understanding of our eyes, be enlightened to the God that we serve, that is more than our savior. He is our keeper. He is our strength. He is our power, power that worketh in us mightily.

> *For by grace are ye saved through faith; and that not of yourselves: it is the gift of God: not of works,*

That means our own works, which are filthy rags in the eyes of God, but the works of God, you see.

> *not of works, lest any man should boast.*

We have nothing to boast in, but we have everything to boast of in the Lord.

> *For we are his workmanship,*

He is working it out in us.

*For we are his workmanship, created in Christ
Jesus unto good works,*

Not our own works, not of works, of our own that is, lest
any man should boast, but we are the workmanship of God
Almighty, the Father. Don't you see? Verse 10, let me read
it again.

*For we are his workmanship, created in Christ
Jesus unto good works, which God hath before
ordained that we should walk in them.*

Walk in what? In the good works of God that only he can
work out in us and through us by the power of the Holy
Ghost that worketh in us mightily. Do not deny him access
to your complete being.

God wants to work; He wants to work a mighty work in
each one of you. Bless his holy name, for you're special.
Each person is unique in the eyes of God. It's his
workmanship. You are created in him that he might work
his mighty works through you. Bless his holy name.

Verse 11,

*Wherefore remember, that ye being in time past
Gentiles in the flesh,*

That means walking in the flesh, saying, I can't help it. And
God knows we could not help but sin because we were in
the fallen nature of the first man, Adam. But now we are
created in Christ by God, we are his workmanship to carry
out his true work of holiness, righteousness, and truth.
We're to walk in his truth.

Wherefore remember, that ye being in time past Gentiles in the flesh, who are called Uncircumcision by that which is called the Circumcision in the flesh made by hands; that at that time ye were without Christ,

Think back, well, you couldn't help but sin without being born again,

being aliens from the commonwealth of Israel, and strangers from the covenants of promise, having no hope, and without God in the world:

Thank God for Jesus. He says,

but now in Christ Jesus,

now precious ones, the moment that you were born again,

but now in Christ Jesus ye who sometimes were far off are made nigh by the blood of Christ.

You've been brought close to God by the blood of Christ Jesus. And he says, for he is our peace, just what the world is looking for. We possess Christ Jesus, the Prince of Peace,

For he is our peace, who hath made both one, and hath broken down the middle wall of partition between us; having abolished in his flesh the enmity, even the law of commandments contained in ordinances; for to make in himself of twain one new man,

We're one in Christ.

so making peace,

see sin will bring enmity, sin will bring separation, sin will destroy a beautiful relationship. But Jesus broke it down, the middle wall of partition, and he's given us access to the throne of God to come into the presence of the most high God through Jesus Christ in his name.

Over in the fourth chapter of Hebrews,

> *Let us therefore fear, lest, a promise being left us of entering into his rest,*

That means His peace,

> *any of you should seem to come short of it. For unto us was the gospel preached, as well as unto them: but the word preached did not profit them, not being mixed with faith in them that heard it.*

See, we must have faith to believe every word that proceeds out of the mouth of God.

> *For we which have believed do enter into rest, as he said,*
>
> *As I have sworn in my wrath,*
>
> *If they shall enter into my rest:*
>
> *although the works were finished from the foundation of the world.*

See, God, seeing the end from the beginning, as far as he was concerned, the work of our salvation was already completed.

He knows them that are his, and he says, let everyone that name it the name of the Lord depart from iniquity. You have to see sin as a gross enemy that it is, and it's a robber, it's a thief to rob you of God's glory and God's expectations of you and of me. Verse four,

> *for he spake in a certain place of the seventh day on this wise, and God did rest the seventh day from all his works.*

> *For he spake in a certain place of the seventh day on this wise, And God did rest the seventh day from all his works. And in this place again,*

> *If they shall enter into my rest.*

> *Seeing therefore it remaineth that some must enter therein, and they to whom it was first preached entered not in because of unbelief: again, he limiteth a certain day, saying in David, To day, after so long a time; as it is said,*

> *To day if ye will hear his voice,*

> *Harden not your hearts.*

God has me going back into this, you might have a greater understanding.

> *For if Jesus had given them rest, then would he not afterward have spoken of another day. There remaineth therefore a rest to the people of God. For he that is entered into his rest, he also hath ceased from his own works,*

See what God is saying in Ephesians chapter two, not of works, that means our own works.

And he says, in Christ, we have ceased from our own works, and we are brought unto God for God to work out his great plan in us. There remaineth therefore a rest to the people of God. In verse 11,

> *Let us labour therefore to enter into that rest, lest any man fall after the same example of unbelief.*

You must believe that God is able to keep you day and night preserved unto himself. God is able; he has the power to do it, but he needs your cooperation. He needs your love, your obedience, your commitment.

He needs you to put your trust completely in him. And as you do so, God will show you how mighty he is in your life. And you will be surprised how God is going to use you as you surrender your all, you commit your way unto the Lord, and he will direct your path, night and day.

Hearing From God

First Aired Sept 30th, 2001

We are in a sobering time, our nation and parts of the world, because of the latest events that have occurred in New York City and the Pentagon. But we praise the Lord for his goodness and his mercies because God is always good and everything that God will ever do or has ever done, it has been for the goodness of man because he is good and he's always concerned about the souls of men, that's why he sent Jesus Christ, his only begotten son, as the savior of this world.

Jesus is the answer to every man's problems, for every man's woes. In the book of Malachi, chapter 2, I'll begin reading at the fifth verse. He's talking to his priest, in the very first verse, he said,

> *And now, O ye priests, this commandment is for you.*

And the reason God is speaking in such a manner through the prophet Malachi to the shepherds, who are called priests, is because the Lord has anointed, has ordained ministers of the gospel to tell the people the truth. I have listened, listening to the radio, listening and looking at television, reading the papers, and I've been listening, watching, and praying. The Lord tells us to watch and pray.

And this I have been doing. And God has moved on many people because of the occurrences of the last few weeks. The bombing of the World Trade Center and the Pentagon, and the plane that went down in Pennsylvania.

Many have been asking why. And I have been listening to the answers. Some have said they don't know why. These are shepherds. And others have stated their opinions. But dear ones, that's not quite what God is after.

We should have a ready answer, a ready answer to the needs of mankind. As Christians, as born-again Christians, we have the answer to the whys. And if we don't, it's because we have not been in the presence of God Almighty, as Christians should be, especially Christian leaders.

The very first verse, chapter 2 of Malachi,

> *And now, O ye priests, this commandment is for you. If ye will not hear, and if ye will not lay it to heart, to give glory unto my name, saith the LORD of hosts, I will even send a curse upon you, and I will curse your blessings: yea, I have cursed them already, because ye do not lay it to heart.*

I've heard ministers preaching, myself included. Second Chronicles 7,

> *if my people, which are called by my name, shall humble themselves, and pray, and seek my face,*

And many have left out this phrase,

> *and turn from their wicked ways.*

The Lord said,

> *and turn from their wicked ways; then will I hear
> from heaven, and will forgive their sin, and will
> heal their land.*

And we all know that we need a visitation from God as never before. I heard one speaking in favor of God. Telling the nation and telling the world on television, that when God lifts his hands of protection, when he removes his hands of protection, over the people or over the nation or over a person, then tragedy happens. Destruction comes. God always desired to bless mankind, and to govern over mankind… to protect.

But we cannot abuse the love of God and take him for granted. That he's a God of love and mercy. And not a God of reproof. God is a God of reproof. And God has feelings. Everyone has been worried about how others feel. But you must understand, I've been ministering for several years on this particular station. And I have been exalting God Almighty to you. Telling you what God feels. That he has emotions. That he feels like we feel. That's where we get our feelings from.

Our soul comes from God. Our spirit comes from God. God can be hurt like anyone else. God gave his only begotten Son that whosoever would believe on him should not perish. One would say, well, many perished at the World Trade Center. No, many died. But perishing is being completely destroyed from the presence of God Almighty. And only God can answer that.

God knows who was his. But the Lord God allowed this shaking to come. To show us our weaknesses, to show us our sins, to show us what we lack of God Almighty. We say, God bless America. One nation under God. But are we as a nation under his divine ordinance? The answer is no…no.

In verse 5 of chapter 2,

> *My covenant was with him of life and peace;*

My covenant was with him of life and peace. God is talking about the priests. Or the shepherds, pastors.

> *and I gave them to him for the fear wherewith he feared me, and was afraid before my name.*

How many have reverenced God in such a manner? Men speak their own words in the name of God. In the name of Christianity. In the name of Jesus. And yet have not sought his counsel. We want to give the people what they want to hear. Instead of what they have need of. He said, verse 6,

> *The law of truth was in his mouth, and iniquity was not found in his lips: he walked with me in peace and equity, and did turn many away from iniquity. For the priest's lips should keep knowledge,*

Ministers of the gospel, of the Lord God Almighty and His Son Jesus Christ, our lips should keep knowledge. It should be in our hearts and in our minds. And our lips, our tongues, should be ready to speak the knowledge of God.

What law? The law of righteousness, the law of truth. The law of divine love. The law of justice. Speaking against sin. Speaking on the behalf of God.

> *or the priest's lips should keep knowledge, and they should seek the law at his mouth: for he is the messenger of the LORD of hosts.*

He is the messenger of the Lord of hosts. I heard one minister say. People are preaching, they are preaching, they are preaching. But the people are hurting. And we just want to heal you. And then they went on to exalt their name and their ministry. Who are you kidding?

If you love the souls of mankind, you will tell them the truth. Only the truth sets one at liberty. The truth makes free. And Jesus is the truth. He said,

> *But ye are departed out of the way; ye have caused many to stumble at the law; ye have corrupted the covenant of Levi, saith the LORD of hosts.*

You have corrupted the covenant…Many are failing. But if ever was the time that ministers of the gospel of Jesus Christ should be in their closets and on the altars of the churches, or wherever you go to seek God, it is now. It is now!

God is letting us know as a nation that we need his divine protection. That all of our military power, and all the fine minds of education. And all of these mighty and glorious things are not enough. We need the mind of Christ. We need the help of God. We need God's protection over our nation.

Yes, we have done many great things as a nation. To all humanity. Millions and billions of dollars have been sent forth to help others that are lacking. But God knows, and he is weighing the hearts of each one of us. From our leaders of the past all the way down to now.

God has been reckoning with America. He has sent many wise men to the capital. To speak "What thus said the Lord."

But how many have taken heed? How many have listened to the wisdom and the knowledge of God? And where are the shepherds? Those who are on the forefront, or rather, those who are readily seen by the public? Where is your backbone in Christ?

Why aren't you abiding in the full armor of God? Why don't you know his mind? Why won't you give the people what they have need of?

Yes, take them in your arms, love them, care for them, weep over them. And speak the truth in love, (tell them) that God Almighty is offended, because this nation has tried to do it without the help of God.

You cannot live without God. This nation was founded on faith in God, as a people from other shores. But God is listening. Because he's merciful. God is waiting to hear this nation repent. This is only a little shaking. Are we going to tell God not to allow any more shaking? Will we repent when we see the error of our ways? (will we say) Have mercy upon us. When we call for prayer. God is looking for someone to repent and turn from wickedness.

The reason God spoke to King Solomon,

> *if my people, which are called by my name, shall humble themselves, and pray, and seek my face, and turn from their wicked ways; then will I hear from heaven, and will forgive their sin, and will heal their land.*

It was because Solomon, in chapter 6 of 2nd Chronicles, was telling God, and repenting about their sins, and telling God of their behavior. And actually, he was praying a priestly prayer then as a king. That wherever the people were in any other part of the world, if they would listen and turn towards Jerusalem and pray and seek forgiveness. He said, "Hear O God, and forgive."

So let's back up from chapter 7. And read what Solomon said to God. In chapter 6. And do likewise. We are not powerful except that the power of God is ruling in our nation, ruling in the churches, ruling in the homes, ruling in the government… ruling!

And God is not like man. That's why we must seek his face. Seek to know what the ways of God are, and what's on his mind. It's time to truly break now, America. We need God's help. And we need to accept the way of the Lord. We are to respect every man. We are to treat every man with dignity, no matter what. But when it comes down to religion. We are to choose the true religion, Jesus Christ!

He is not defiled…He's pure, and He's holy. And get this, He is the only way to salvation. He's the only way to life and peace. When Jesus came preaching, He said: "Repent, for the kingdom of heaven is at hand!"

Religion will take you as far as this life and the mysteries of the spirit world. But Jesus will take you to eternal life and into the most high Heaven where He and the Father dwell forevermore.

After death is the judgment, and this is what we shepherds had better realize, and better tell the people. We do not embrace…we may respect other religions. But we have the truth: Jesus is the way!

And we shepherds, and we Christians will have to answer to God. As to what we have done with humanity in speaking the truth or hiding our lights under a bushel. We can't afford, we cannot afford to pat people on the back. We've got to tell them the truth, and then pat them on the back.

Many preachers are failing God through this time of great sorrow. People need the truth…you are not the savior, Jesus is! Speak the truth. How did you get born again? It was because you heard the truth. You must be born again, or you cannot enter into the kingdom of heaven.

Don't you know that after death there is a heaven and there is a hell? Many will stand before Jesus Christ with the blood of souls on their hands, so we have to choose. Who are we really going to serve? Are we the servants of the Lord God Almighty and his son Jesus Christ? Or are we going to dictate to Him what we want him to do?

No, the word is written, it's on record. The Lord said,

> *I will go before thee, and make the crooked places straight:*

Isaiah 45. Chapter verse 2,

> *I will break in pieces the gates of brass, and cut in sunder the bars of iron:*

The Lord knows how to break yokes. He knows how to set the captives free. He knows how, as a glorious Father of love, to protect his own. God desires to protect America. And all other nations under the sun. But America is more responsible before God than any other nation. Because we are the greater blessed. And to whom much is given, much is required.

God is holding us accountable. I love America; I was born here. I have traveled to other nations, and I have been so happy to get back to my own nation. Because, as far as I know and as far as I have witnessed, there is no other nation like America, the United States of America, under the sun.

But yet, God is looking on the sins of America. We are poor right here in America. In dire need of help. Ask Larry Jones, Feed the Children Ministry. Many people, many people have gone to prison, and died, and were not guilty. Because of the injustice of the system. And many more will.

And God is visiting America. Did God bomb the World Trade Center? He did not. But he allowed America to see.

If he pulled his hand back. Like my brother said. And turn us over to the enemy of our souls… God and God alone can protect us. And if he turns us over, there is nothing but destruction in the land.

Look at the fires. Look at the floods. Look at the storms. And now this. I speak on the behalf of God, my Father. I speak on the behalf of God the Son, my Savior and my friend, and Lord. By the power of the Holy Ghost that He has entrusted in me to speak the truth with a spiritual backbone. And I speak it in love. Because I care for the souls of humanity.

It's time to get right with God. America. The Lord said in verse 5,

> *I am the LORD, and there is none else, there is no God beside me: I girded thee, though thou hast not known me: that they may know from the rising of the sun, and from the west, that there is none beside me. I am the LORD, and there is none else. I form the light, and create darkness: I make peace, and create evil: I the LORD do all these things.*

God does it. And in verse 22,

> *Look unto me, and be ye saved, all the ends of the earth: for I am God, and there is none else.*

> *I have sworn by myself, the word is gone out of my mouth in righteousness, and shall not return, That unto me every knee shall bow, every tongue shall swear. Surely, shall one say, in the LORD have I*

The Lord our righteousness. The Lord our King. Jesus said. In Saint John 14.

 The children of God are not afraid. We see and understand, and know what's happening and why. And we should readily tell others. Even if they bark at the truth, the truth will follow them. For the Lord said, "My word shall not return unto me void."

Maybe eventually they will receive the truth. But it's our duty to speak it on the behalf of God and the souls of men, and yet, for ourselves also in Jesus name.

It's time for this nation to bend our knees and break in our spirits and become hearts of flesh that we can be molded and shaped according to the will of God. Or else there are penalties to be paid. God is our help. Jesus Christ, the resurrection and the power of God. Those who have gone on, if they died in Christ, are home in glory before him.

What about you? Think on these things. In Jesus name we pray. Amen.

Listen to the Podcast

Listen to Evangelist Martha P. Davis today at your favorite podcast location. Just look for God's Holy Mountain Broadcast, or scan below: